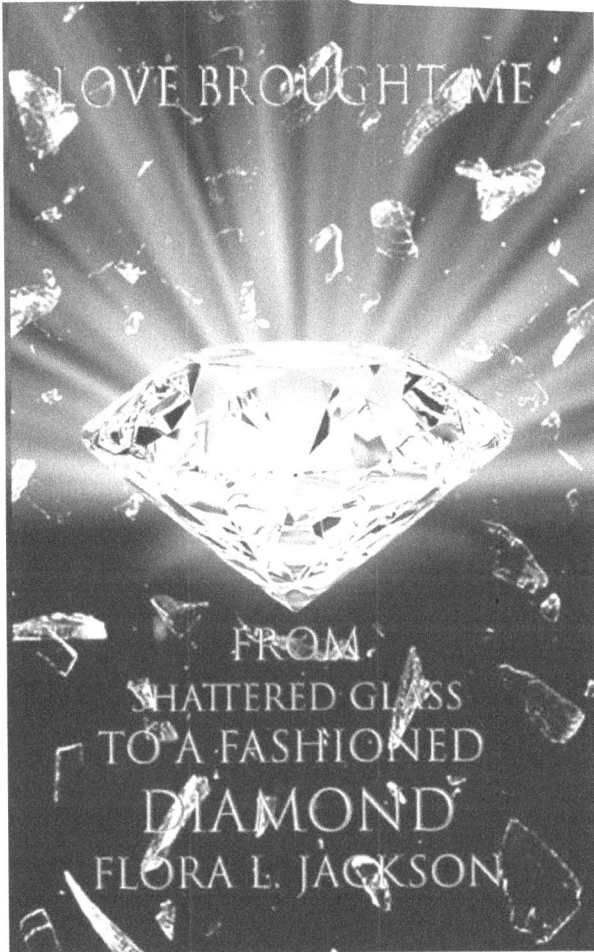

LOVE BROUGHT ME

FROM
SHATTERED GLASS
TO A FASHIONED
DIAMOND
FLORA L. JACKSON

By

Flora L. Jackson

LOVE BROUGHT ME: FROM SHATTERED GLASS TO A FASHIONED DIAMOND

Cover Designed by Robert Camren Cates
Author's Photo: Roosevelt Foster's Work of Art

ISBN: 9798987180501
Library of Congress: 2023910015

The disclaimer: The opinions and views expressed in this book are that of the author.

For information, write to the publisher:
Love Overflowing Publishing
Lovebroughtme@yahoo.com
Facebook: Love Overflowing Publishing

Chicago, Illinois

DEDICATION

To the many hearts of all ages and all genders who have been broken and shattered by a devastating experience in their lives! You may have thought you would never recover from that unpleasant event. But I am a witness that there is hope, help, and healing available to transform your life! You can be designed into something radiantly beautiful as a 'Fashioned Diamond!'

The Diamond Cutter's hands are well capable of tenderly and carefully fashioning (you) the precious stone. He is aware of the value he holds in his hands. God is the skilled Diamond Cutter! He does not throw away any part of the priceless GEM, because He knows your worth!

You Are a Valued Person

You Are a Priceless Gem

You Are a Precious Jewel and

You Are Loved Beyond Measure

CONTENTS

ACKNOWLEDGMENTS

Special thanks to my first family, my two daughters Andrea and Shawn, for picking up the torch and teaching their children the value of having a loving and personal relationship with Jesus Christ. This is the best gift to any mother: knowing that your children love the Lord and are teaching their children to love the Lord!

Thanks to my youngest grandson, Camren, for working with me on the cover. I am overjoyed by the way you were able to capture my thoughts. To my grandchildren and great-grandchildren, you have captured my heart. Grammy loves you dearly and always!

Also, an extraordinary special thanks to my wonderful heavenly family, the people who laid the foundation for this book: Grandmother Virgie (Granny), Elnora (Mom), Richard (Dad), and Jerry (my one and only sibling). I called her my one-in-a-million because she liked money.

Next, I want to thank to my spiritual family, Love Overflowing Ministries, for your awesome example and display of love, unity, and support of Flora L. Jackson, aka "Mama J" or Prophetess Jackson.

To Pastors Marque and Lisa Shaffer, thanks for the help, support, and encouragement to see this project through. We are a great team; love is definitely in the mix! Also, to Minister Toni Harris, who became my eyes and did most of the editing, words are not enough to express my gratitude. And thanks to Dr. Robert L. Watts, for pushing me to complete an assignment that was well overdue.

Special thanks to my prayer warriors, aka "God's Glorious Gospel Gangsters," which is a nickname we picked up because of so many answered prayers in spiritual warfare! And thanks to all the supporting prayer intercessors from: Milwaukee WI, Dallas TX, Meridianville AL, Mather CA, Normal IL, Chicago IL, and the suburbs. I feel your prayers daily!

Finally and graciously, to my Lord and Savior, Jesus Christ, for choosing me and giving me the strength to complete this blessed work for His glory!

FOREWORD

Flora L. Jackson has ministered, mentored, and counseled thousands of people throughout her many years in ministry. Saved as a teenager, she says, "I came to Christ out of fear, but I stayed because of love!"

Her love for God and people has transformed the lives of countless individuals through formal ministry, street witnessing, Bible teaching, years of media ministry, and personal interaction.

Flora, or "Mama J", as she is affectionately known, has witnessed several generations of her family come into the saving grace of Jesus Christ. And scores of adoptive children now walk in the faith. God has blessed her to see all five-fold ministries come forth from her: by direct prayer, mentoring, prophesying, healing, deliverance, encouragement, friendship, and by godly example to all she meets.

She is currently the founder and leader of **"Love Overflowing Ministries"** (LOM), a parachurch ministry that draws people in from different churches and denominations. LOM began in 2006 and has set out to "Reveal and Fulfill the Love of God to Mankind," which is our motto. Mama J's message to the church is: *"IF WE CAN GET THE LOVE RIGHT, WE CAN GET THE WORLD RIGHT!"* God has used LOM, as he has in every ministry Mama J has served, to transform lives for the glory of God.

Now this book will allow others to be inspired, challenged, and encouraged to understand God's love for them a little more clearly, so that they can love Him a little more dearly.

By Pastor Marque Shaffer (Member and Associate Pastor of LOM)

INTRODUCTION

This book is intended to reach those who have been through heartbreaking, earth-shaking, and life-shattering events! The pressure you endured may have destroyed your hope for a bright future. But I know from personal experience that one moment can change your life—for the rest of your life, for the better! You will be healed as you see things through the eyes of the one who was **Shattered to Pieces!**

Within the confines of this book, the author will take you on a compelling journey of truth about how she was shattered while desperately needing to be loved!

***People need to know that love is not a feeling; it is a happening*!** Love can transform your life in a moment! Love will draw you to a place of healing, trust, comfort, and freedom! You will sense a love that is neither judgmental nor condemning. But you will find true love in the midst of these pages, which will have you seeking for more!

For the first time in years, the author finally gets to tell her story in detail. You will experience the magnificence of every little detail of how the shattered pieces were put back together! As the Master Craftsman is creating, sculpting, and fashioning, he sees a great and radiant brilliance coming from the crevices of the diamond! The deeper the cut, the greater the quality and worth of the diamond, as the beauty shines through!

Flora L. Jackson has had the opportunity to tell her story in different parts of America. She has evangelized and ministered for years, from the East Coast to the West Coast. However, "Telling Her Story has never been shared in detail, until now! You will read and experience the glory of the story in this book titled, **"Love Brought Me: From Shattered Glass to a Fashioned Diamond!"**

TELLING MY STORY

If I don't tell my story, who will?

If I don't share the glory, who will?

If I don't talk about my journey, who will?

If I don't speak about my miracles, who will?

If I don't articulate my personal feelings, who will?

If I don't communicate my love to others, who will?

If I don't open my mouth and praise my God, then who will?

BY: Flora L. Jackson

CHAPTER ONE

MY STORY

LIFE IS ABOUT CHOICES

Come stroll with me through the corridors of time as I share vulnerable events that ultimately changed my life instantly and forever. I've learned to never take a moment for granted.

My story begins as ordinary, but if you don't stay until the end, you will miss the extraordinary glory!

I was raised going to church from my childhood. My family attended the Baptist church, the Catholic church, and the Pentecostal church all at the same time while digesting multiple forms of theology.

We went to the Baptist church because that's where my mother preferred to go and where most of her friends also attended. My mom was very popular, as she was involved in numerous activities such as the choir, the plays, and every fundraiser you can imagine. We went to the Catholic church faithfully because my sister and I attended the Catholic school in the neighborhood. The school's requirements were to take Catholic-related studies and attend Mass services as part of the curriculum.

We also attended the Pentecostal church because my grandmother was insistent that we attend, even if it was just to take her to church. My mother would not deny her because Grandma used to keep us while my mom went to work. However, taking her to church and picking her up every week became an ongoing challenge. So many times, we simply stayed at her church to keep the cost of traveling down. It seemed that the more we took Grandma to the Pentecostal church, the less time we had to attend the Baptist church.

Eventually, we moved from the neighborhood where my sister and I attended the Catholic school and church. As time passed, we were only attending church with my grandmother. Somehow, I think Grandma had a plan all along, and it was working. Soon, my family became more and more involved with the Pentecostal Church. Need I say again that I was raised going to church since my childhood?

One day, a revival meeting came to the little storefront Pentecostal church. My mom and dad repented of their sins and confessed that they were **Born Again.** We had always been a part of the fabric of the church, but this was different. Something had changed! Both of them had accepted Jesus Christ as their Lord and Savior. They were totally different people! My parents announced to my sister and me that things were going to be better.

All the years that my parents were faithfully going to church and actively participating in church, they had never surrendered their lives to the Lord. This brings a thought to my mind, which the pastor used to say, "That coming to church does not make you a Christian any more than going into a garage makes you a car!"

When my parents accepted Jesus, I was 10 years old, and my sister was 15 years old. Truly, things did change for the better. Our home was more peaceful; their bad habits stopped, and the arguing and sometimes fighting stopped. There was just a different spirit in our home. I couldn't explain it, but I tell you, I truly felt it!

Shortly after my parents' conversion, my sister Jerry accepted Jesus Christ as her personal Savior. I learned that she had become friends with a group of Christians at the new high school. My sister was so excited about her *born again* experience! Jerry seemed to be very spiritually motivated by her Christian friends. They would call her and encourage her daily. Now my sister had become a different person, just as my parents.

One Sunday, while attending the little storefront Pentecostal church, the pastor asked for all the youth to come to the front of the church and stand near the altar (which was just the podium). I was standing in the midst of the crowd of young people that came forward.

Then I heard Pastor ask a most heart-wrenching

question. He asked, "How many of you want to die and go to hell? Raise your hand!"

Of course, none of us raised our hands.

I thought, "Who wants to die and go to hell?"

Then I heard Pastor ask another question, and this one was just as compelling as the first. He asked us youth, "How many of you want to be saved and go to heaven?"

Suddenly, all of our hands went up!

Then Pastor led us through the prayer of repentance by asking us to repeat after him. We did just as he said. After we finished the prayer, he told us we were saved!

He then told the prayer team to come and pray for us and to lay hands on us. The prayer team encouraged each of us to tell Jesus, *"Thank you for saving me!"*

As I followed their instructions, I felt light and started jumping around because I felt like rejoicing! In my church, they called this action the "Holy Dance" or "Shouting," which was simply rejoicing. Wow! I was now confessing to being saved at 10 years old. All I really understood was the rejoicing part, and I continued to rejoice in most services.

We were also encouraged to testify at every service. The pattern of words that was instilled in us went like this: "I thank God for being saved, sanctified, and filled with the precious Holy Ghost, and that with a mighty burning fire!" What a powerful confession for a child who had barely been saved for a week.

My family continued to be faithful in the work of the Lord. My mom was teaching and directing the choir, my dad played the drums, my sister played the organ, and I led most of the choir songs. We were willing workers for the church and for the Lord.

TRYING TO FIT IN EVERYWHERE

Even though I was in the church, I soon found out that the church was not yet in me! I was loyal to my confession of being a Christian. However, I really did not know the true meaning of being a Christian at that time in my life. Yes, I knew right from wrong, and I lived in that manner. My desire to sing in the choir, to testify, and to rejoice on Sunday was still in me. I enjoyed myself at church!

However, I was the same crazy, fun-loving Flora on Monday! When I went to school or hung around my friends in the neighborhood, I enjoyed being with them too! We always seemed to have so much fun.

I knew the scriptures very well. But when the pastor would quote scriptures at church like *(2 Corinthians*

6:17) "Come out from among them and be ye separate, said the Lord." I believed that scripture was for those who were sinning, but not for me. In my mind, I wasn't sinning; I was just having fun with my unsaved friends!

As I grew older, I developed a pattern that helped me fit in everywhere. I would fit in with my Christian friends on Sunday, who were not that much different from my unsaved, worldly friends. But on Monday, I would fit right in with my worldly friends at school. I was doing what they did because I thought it was just me, simply being my fun-loving self.

I adapted to this lifestyle so well that I did not have a clue that I was training myself to be a hypocrite! I adjusted my behavior by trying to fit in on all sides. So, in reality, I was not all bad, and I was not all good! I did not know that my strategy was a dangerous state of mind to be in spiritually! I did not know my position was causing me to be lukewarm, as described in *(Revelation 3:16)* because being lukewarm is a state of being that God does not approve of.

By the time I was 14 years old, I was really good at hiding the bad and the ugly stuff from my family.

My mom would say things like, *"You cannot straddle the fence! You cannot serve two masters."*

(Luke 16:13) Then she would say, "You've got to make up your mind as to who you will serve!"

Because of my lack of commitment to God and my truly not serving him alone, I was being enticed deeper into worldliness.

VULNERABLE TO WORLDLINESS

I would like to share a quote that the Lord gave to me as an adult: it says, "Every day you are not growing into godliness is a day you are vulnerable and open to worldliness!" My choices had me blindsided by my own lust or curiosity for sin, and I was slowly drifting away from God!

I did not understand just how vulnerable I was. I wanted to fit in and be accepted so badly that I had brain fog and could not see the pit I was about to fall into!

I know now that 14 is a pivotal and dangerous age! After some recent research, I found facts that agree with me. In my youth, I was searching for my own direction and mindset, which always seemed to be different from what I was taught. I did not realize that the friends I thought so much of were having the same identity crisis too.

Friendships at that age seem to be the epitome of all happiness, fun, and a good time, and without them, life can seem dull and boring.

However, the reality of life was about to hit me right between the eyes! I was exposed to more worldliness than I was used to, so I picked up some bad habits. I started cussing, lying, talking disrespectfully, and criticizing other people at the expense of their feelings just to make my *toxic friends* laugh. I was doing things I knew my parents would not be proud of, yet I kept this side of me hidden from them. More and more, I was becoming like that bad news group that I was hanging with. I even told myself that being bad was liberating and fun. All of this nonsense was about me trying to be like them just so I could fit in and be accepted.

But through all of this big, bad, bold talking and acting tough, *I never disrespected my parents, which is why I am alive today and able to tell my story!* My mother was not always saved, and I had enough experience and common sense to know to watch my mouth because she did not play!

CHOOSING THE WRONG FRIENDS

My family had no idea I had lost my mind to the influence of the streets. My mindset was slowly turning away from the church and from God.

My mentors now became the older neighborhood teens, and young adults from the toxic group of friends who had no desire for God or the church. But they had my attention!

I started making excuses about going to church,

choir rehearsal, or any events that had to do with the church. I didn't want to sing anymore. So I started hiding in the background, hoping no one would suggest I sing or participate.

PLEASE LET ME TAKE A PAUSE HERE:

Parents, when your children say they no longer want to go to church or if they ask you why they have to go, STOP everything and please pay attention to what they are saying! They are telling you that something or someone has their attention! Don't ignore them! This is the time to have a one-on-one "Talk and Listen" session with them. (John 10:10) "The thief comes to steal, to kill, and to destroy." Satan is that thief, and he wants your children. But God has a master plan to rescue them!

BACK TO MY STORY:

I did not know exactly what was going on in my mind except that I was looking for my own identity, and I thought I could find it in my relationship with these friends. I felt some kind of bond and boldness while with them. However, I was on the wrong course. This truly was not the way, yet I persisted on this path.

I personally learned the hard way that deception and lying will steer you down the wrong path to a quick demise and utter destruction!

I was determined to have a future with these unruly,

rowdy characters. We had just graduated and would be attending high school together. We had partnered and agreed on our plans. We were going to have a ball! Some of the older teens with a stronger influence on us were already students at the high school, and they were just waiting for us all to hook up so they could show us the ropes.

I thought to myself, "Finally, I will get the chance to be with these crazy, fun-loving friends even more than usual." We talked about our plans to be in different organizations and be associated with some of the popular after-school clubs. We also planned the different activities that we all wanted to be a part of as we prepared to attend high school together, *and our plans were set!*

DOES GOD LAUGH AT OUR PLANS?

But with all my plans, guess what? I was not in control of anything, not even my own life. It seemed just as I was starting to fit in with that riotous crowd, the rug was pulled right out from under me!

When I came home one evening, Jerry and my parents were just sitting down to eat dinner. My parents said they wanted to speak with us about something very serious. Then suddenly, what they said totally rocked my world! They told us that we were moving!

What? I could not believe what I was hearing! I was shocked and quite devastated!

My parents happily shared the news that they had purchased their own house! I remember how excited they were to share this news with us because we were living in an apartment building! Then the next thing they told us was just as devastating to me when they said, "We are moving across town to the west side of Chicago!" Things seemed to get worse with every sentence. Finally, they concluded with a powerful punchline by saying, "And we will be moving in two weeks!"

I just could not believe this was happening to me! I was going to be attending a high school where I didn't know anyone! Jerry was calm because she had already graduated and was in a successful work program. So, the news did not affect her at all. At this point, all *my plans* were gone down the drain, thrown out the window, and completely dismissed! *(Proverbs 16:9) A man's heart plans his way...*

I was so hurt! My mom truly felt sorry for me; she understood that the transition would be tough on the family. I could not understand why God would let this happen to me! I was going to have to leave my south side neighborhood, all my friends who I cared so much about, and everything that had become so familiar to me.

I didn't know how I was going to tell my friends that I was moving. My spirit was broken at the thought of leaving. Finally, after a few days, I got the opportunity to tell them the awful, sad news!

Reluctantly, I shared the painful news with my friends that I was moving out of the neighborhood to the west side of Chicago. Next, I sadly shared with them that I would be moving within the next couple of weeks.

I DID NOT GET THE RESPONSE I EXPECTED!

Those fun-loving friends that I was trying to move heaven and earth to be with, you know? The ones that I wanted to be like said, "Oh well, see yah! Goodbye, I wouldn't want to be yah!" After that, they walked away laughing!

Instantly, I was heartbroken! How cold can you be to a friend?

Those ruthless characters, whom I called friends, dropped me like a hot potato! I felt disrespected and disconnected all at the same time!

I was left standing there dismayed and shocked at the lack of any concern or caring from the ones that I thought were my friends! I had thought it was cool hanging with these loud-mouthed, crazy friends who had no boundaries. We talked about people saying ugly, harmful things. At the time, I was not sensitive to what we did to hurt other people—until it happened to me!

Then I had an epiphany! A sudden revelation hit me in a moment! My eyes were opened, and I got a life lesson right then and there. I learned that I had placed too much value on their friendship and that they were not my friends at all! When I looked back in my mind's eye, I could see how things had been one-sided all along. I could see how they used me to do stupid, crazy things for their pleasure and entertainment while secretly laughing behind my back. What I once thought was a fun-loving bunch of friends, I then saw as disrespectful, foul-mouthed, obnoxious teens. This group would do or say anything to anybody, especially for a joke or a laugh.

All of a sudden, I could see how I had been played like a fiddle! And used by my so-called friends. What a painful eye-opener!

Yes, I was overwhelmingly hurt and felt like a fool, to say the least! But I had no choice but to pick myself up and carry on.

Thank God, I had other friends in the neighborhood. However, I didn't realize that I had turned to them to try to fill the rejection from my bad news friends.

Yet I was still looking for love and acceptance because it meant so much to me to be connected.

GOD'S TIMING IS EVERYTHING

Now, as I look back, it seems ironic how God used my grandmother to influence the plans and choices that my parents made. It was those choices that led my parents to be ***Born Again!***

Also, I see how God used my parents' plans and choices to move away from the old neighborhood at *the right time*, just before I was about to bust loose with the wrong crowd! I did not see God's plan in the midst of the heartache and heartbreak! ***But I am a witness that God's plans and His timing are everything!***

(Jeremiah 29:11) "For I know the plans I have for you, says the LORD. They are plans for good and not for disaster, to give you a future and a hope."

PERSONAL REFLECTIONS CONCERNING CHAPTER 1

This may be my story, but maybe you can relate to the situations from a different time, location, and with different people. Here are some thoughts to ponder:

1. Are you looking for love and acceptance in all the wrong places? Stop and reflect!

2. Who are you trying to impress by being someone you are not, just to fit in?

3. What are you hiding from your family and those who love you?

4. Examine yourself! Are you making the right choices for your best future?

5. Do you attend church? Are there personal reasons why you attend church or do not attend church?

6. Who is the greatest influence in your life?

SCRIPTURE REFERENCE FOR CHAPTER ONE

All scripture is taken from the King James Version Bible unless otherwise noted.

2 Corinthians 6:17
Wherefore come out from among them and be ye separate, said the Lord. And touch not the unclean thing; and I will receive you.

Revelation 3:15-16
I know your works, that you are neither cold nor hot. I could wish you were cold or hot. 16 So then, because you are lukewarm and neither cold nor hot, I will vomit you out of my mouth. NKJV

Luke 16:13
No servant can serve two masters: for either he will hate the one and love the other, or else he will hold to the one and despise the other.

John 10:10
The thief cometh not, but for to steal, and to kill, and to destroy; I am come that they might have life, and that they might have it more abundantly.

Proverbs 16:9
A man's heart plans his way, But the LORD directs his steps. NKJV

Jeremiah 29:11
For I know the plans I have for you, says the
LORD. They are plans for good and not for disaster,
to give you a future and a hope. NLT

CHAPTER TWO

SHATTERED GLASS

TRYING TO SOOTHE THE PAIN

Although I was hurt and disappointed about the loss and rejection of my potential high school buddies, I wisely accepted the fact that they really were not my friends.

However, I had other friends. We grew up together in the neighborhood, riding our bikes and playing ball in the vacant lot. These were my nerdy friends; they just wanted to act like they were older, do silly things, and try things they had never done before. It was this group of friends that my parents trusted and allowed me to be with because they had known their families for years.

By now, I was attending high school on the west side of Chicago. My mom and I had implemented a plan, along with the help of my childhood friend,

Joyce, and her mother. The plan was that on the days my mom would be on the south side, I would leave home early and ride the bus to the old neighborhood. Then, at the designated time, my mom would pick me up from Joyce's house. This plan of action did not happen every day, just on special dates or events. My mom really tried hard to keep me connected with friends as much as possible since we had moved so far away. The whole idea was for me to spend some quality time with Joyce and familiar faces since I didn't know anyone on the west side.

Mom had already planned for our family to attend the New Year's Eve service at the storefront Pentecostal church. We continued going to the same church on the south side, even though we had moved to the west side. So, we still had reasons to come around occasionally. The church was located in the old neighborhood near Joyce's house, which made it most convenient.

The New Year's Eve service was a tradition to pray the old year out and pray the new year in. Since the service did not start until 11:30 p.m., Joyce and I would have plenty of leisure time before my mom would arrive to pick me up for service.

PIVOTAL IDENTITY CRISIS

On that particular New Year's Eve, Joyce and I had planned to spend the evening with Karen, another friend of ours. At least, that is what Joyce told her mother we were going to do. But she had other plans. Lying to her mother seemed to be totally out of character for her behavior! However, I was surprised when she informed me that we were going to a 17-year-old's birthday party! Now you know that when you are 13 or 14 years old, that age is like light years from the 17 or 18-year-old teens.

Immediately, a red flag went up in my mind. I just did not feel right about doing this adventure. But I didn't say anything to Joyce because I didn't want to spoil her plans. Joyce had already decided that when we arrived at the party, all we needed to do was act older and look older to fit in! As I look back, it seems Joyce was going through the same identity crisis that I was going through. Her desire was to fit in with an older group of teens and to be accepted as well.

We left Joyce's house, pretending to go to our friend Karen's house, which was just a block away. But instead, we headed to the party. It was already nightfall, and I had no idea where we were going. I knew we had walked quite far in the cold to get there. We arrived at the party about 8 p.m. We met with our contact person, who was the younger sister of the birthday girl. Tammy was one of Joyce's classmates. So, we casually sneaked in with her like we belonged.

However, we had no idea what we would be facing before the night was over!

THE RED LIGHT BULB PARTY

I remember coming in the front door, and the room was full of adults passing drinks around to other adults. As we slipped in, they directed us to go downstairs into the basement, where the birthday party was going on. The adults seemed to have started their New Year's Eve celebration upstairs already. So, we timidly and respectfully walked through to where we were directed.

Whew! We made it in with no problem. As we opened the door to the basement, we could barely see anything as we went down the steps. We could hear the music and the voices, but the reason we could not see was because there was only one red light bulb on in the whole basement! It was so utterly dark and red that it took a few minutes for our eyes to adjust. Then, in the midst of the red hue, we could see the party was quite full.

We were shy at first because we didn't know anyone except Joyce's friend, who had sneaked us into the party. But we soon started mingling with some of the others.

Joyce had already invited her boyfriend, Jonathan, who conveniently lived in the neighborhood. But we certainly were not in our neighborhood! We had walked seven or eight long blocks and crossed a couple busy streets to get to this place.

However, things seemed to be going quite well. We were all acting mature, dancing, eating, laughing, talking, and just having a good time.

Joyce jokingly mentioned how we fooled and outsmarted our parents. She even proudly bragged about the different little lies she told to get us to the party. We thought it was funny as we talked about how scary it was getting past the adults upstairs. What a sigh of relief! Our fear of getting caught was over!

We actually laughed at ourselves for pretending to be older, yet we blended in very well with no problem at all. No one seemed to suspect anything. Soon we felt comfortable enough to relax.

Eventually, I took turns dancing with a few of the guys, including Jonathan; he was a good friend and good company too. While enjoying ourselves, we did not realize the time had gone by so quickly. It was already past 10 o'clock!

Of course, my mind started calculating the time remaining before my mom was to pick me up from Joyce's house. Listen, when Mom said to be there at a certain time, she meant it!

I started feeling a little uncomfortable about the time and the distance we'd have to travel to get back to my friend's house. Nevertheless, Joyce assured me we would make it on time and not to worry. So we continued dancing and having fun, but this time we were paying close attention to the clock.

THE HANDS OF DESTRUCTION

Shortly afterwards, Joyce took a needed break and asked me to dance with Jonathan. Even though our eyes had adjusted to the dark red room by then, it was still very intimidating trying to move around to a different spot.

The music changed to a slow beat. Jonathan and I were casually talking while dancing, not paying attention to the noise of the crowd or the new disturbance that had just started around us. We had no idea that the birthday party had been invaded by a gang of about six young men. They had entered the back door to the basement with other teens who were attending the party. Yet at the time, we did not have a clue about what was going on around us.

Suddenly! Out of the blue, someone snatched me from Jonathan's arms aggressively! It happened so quickly and forcefully that my body bumped hard against the body of the person who grabbed me! Mind you, I was a small, short, and lightweight 14-year-old girl. I had on a short, pleated skirt. It felt like I was flying in the air as my skirt ballooned from the force of the wind going underneath. But when that force of motion stopped—impact!!! It felt like I had hit a brick wall, and the breath was literally knocked out of my body! At that point, I could barely breathe! Things happened so fast that I was in a daze from this out-of-control tail spin!

I thought to myself, "Wow! What in the world just happened to me?"

I was trying to mentally figure it out. While still dazed from the impact and not being able to see in the dark red room, I was completely bewildered!

OMG! When I was finally able to comprehend what was actually happening to me, I was totally shocked! I thought, "Who in the world is this big, brawny guy grabbing me, and why is *he* grabbing *me*?"

This maniac proceeded to assault my body, forcibly putting his hands on areas of my body that I objected to him touching! No way was this a dance! He was holding me so tight that I could barely breathe as his body pressed against mine!

He literally towered over me; I was absolutely helpless! I was being molested, harassed, and assaulted in a room full of people, and no one reached out to help me! This brute was physically hurting me, violently squeezing my wrist and twisting my arm behind my back as he whispered ugly things in my ear! The more I fought him off, the stronger he got!

I thought, "Why me? Why did he pick me out? Why is he touching on my body?"

I was very frightened! Nothing like this had ever happened to me before. I started crying and asking for help, but no one came to my rescue! I kept pleading with the bully to let me go!

I said, "Please let me go!" I started to panic at the helplessness I felt! I continued to plead with him, "Please, get your hands off of me!"

I was so terrified that he might have his way with me right there at the party! The more I struggled to get away, the more it seemed to be mere entertainment to him and his friends.

I declare this monster had multiple hands, and they were fast and overpowering with every touch. He was squeezing me so tightly while making advances on my small, innocent body.

As I was frantically fighting him off, all I could think was, "*I am someplace I should not be, being handled by someone I do not know, and my parents don't have any idea where I am!!!*"

OMG! Joyce and I had lied and laughed about outsmarting our parents. Now, I was in a threatening predicament that I could not get out of by myself. I needed help!

While reasoning with myself, fearful and uncertain of what was going to happen, I realized how wrong I had been. I wanted to be with an older crowd, but this was way out of my league. This was *not* the future I wanted for my life!

Out of desperation, I started praying, "God, if you just get me out of this alive, I am going to do the right thing! Lord, please help me, Jesus!"

Then I prayed a more soulful, desperate prayer, saying, *"Lord! If you get me out of this, I will live for you!"* (Psalm 119:146) *I cried out to you; rescue me.*

It seemed to be with this last request that God heard my prayer of desperation. Because immediately, I heard a voice saying, "Let her go; take your hands off of her now!" (*Psalm 34:6*) *In my desperation, I prayed, and the Lord listened.*

The troublemaker that was roughly handling me angrily responded to the voice by saying, "Who do you think you're talking to?" Then he called that person out of his name.

That's when I realized the person he was hollering at was my friend, 14-year-old Jonathan. He was the only hero in the whole room! This young boy boldly stood up to the big, strong bully on my behalf!

You can imagine my relief to know that *someone* in the room cared about what was happening to me! But now Jonathan had put himself in harm's way to help me. Even though he had spoken up, the bully quickly sized up Jonathan's small frame, and he continued to harmfully violate me, and he would not let me go! He had me in a grip like Jaws!

Someone must have finally gone upstairs to get help. A few of the men came down the stairs to find out what the trouble was about. As the adults came into the basement, they could not see what was going on because their eyes had not adjusted to the dark red room. But the assailant was still holding onto me as he defiantly refused to let me go!

However, as a result of the adults coming into the basement, the harasser finally dropped the fierce grip he had on my wrist! Suddenly, the gang started leaving swiftly out the back door. But the bully did not leave before threatening me and Jonathan, telling us we'd better not come outside!

I was so shaken up! I really didn't know if the gang had bothered or threatened anyone else! Nevertheless, even with the bully's frightening threat hanging over our heads, we knew we had to leave because it was already after 11 p.m. I had less than 20 minutes to get to Joyce's house before it was time for my mom to pick me up.

I truly did not want to be disobedient and face the wrath of my mother, especially after the horror I had just experienced! *(Colossians 3:20) Always obey your parents, for this pleases the Lord.*

Now, we had to think about how we were going to get home without being accosted by a gang in the alley! These guys were huge. Need I say that we were all very nervous and afraid?

HEROES COME IN ALL SIZES

Since the adult New Year's Eve party was going strong upstairs, we were told all the teens that had to leave should go out the back door of the basement. The adults did not want us to disturb their party.

Now things were very scary! We did not have a choice but to leave out the back door. We didn't know if the gang was waiting to fulfill the threat or not, but we knew we could not stay there!

The party never returned to normal. We were not the only teens to leave out the back door, but as we did, we saw a few of the gang members in the alley where we had to exit from the back gate.

Fear gripped my heart! Joyce and I were clinging to one another like little girls. Yes, we were shaking in our boots and on the verge of tears! As we nervously entered the gangway to the alley, we trusted Jonathan to help us get away. Now, not only was Jonathan small in stature, he was kind of a nerd as well, *but he had a plan!*

Jonathan said, "As soon as we get to the gate, run as

if our lives depended on it!" He told us to cut through the backyard straight ahead of us because we could see the gang had formed at each end of the alley. The last plan of action he told us was not to stop running until we got home!

Fearfully, we anticipated the moment of our departure as we approached the gate. But as soon as we got to the gate, we noticed the guy who had been threatening us was standing nearby with a *long knife drawn.* And we could see the *shining blade twinkling* under the streetlights in the alley! Frightened and afraid, we didn't have time to assess *the bully's* plan because we were concentrating on implementing *our own* plan!

The last thing I heard Jonathan say in a loud, thunderous voice was, "Ru-u-u-u-u-n-n-n!!!" We immediately took heed to his command! We ran like lightning through backyards with no idea whether the yards had dogs or people in them. We ran with one purpose in mind: *to save our own lives!*

Joyce and I were slinging sweat, snot, and tears all at the same time as we ran with all of our might! I remember never looking back to see if anyone was following us because I was focused on getting us to a safe place.

Yes, we were concerned about Jonathan, but we had to follow the plan of instructions that he had given us for our survival!

We even ran across the busy four-lane street without stopping or looking! We did not stop until we got to Joyce's front porch steps. It must have taken us at least 10–15 minutes to walk those 7-8 long blocks *to* the party, but it only took us about 4-5 minutes or less to run home, non-stop!

AFRAID AND BROKEN

Our hearts were still pounding as we tried to catch our breath. Oh, my God! We had finally made it out of that horrible, terrifying, and scary experience, which seemed like it would never end!

Whew! There was such a strong sense of relief, yet we were still overwhelmed by fear! We nervously started looking around to see if we had been followed. Since we did not see anything to prove that we were being followed, we began trying to calm ourselves down.

We were breathing hard, like we had been in a long race. Our hearts were pounding swiftly in our chests, and our clothes were damp from perspiration. Now we had to take time to pull ourselves together before going into the house, so nobody would have reason to ask us any questions.

Fortunately, Joyce's bedroom was right by the front door, so we entered quietly as she announced to her family that she was home. We went into her room and stopped everything to pray and ask God to protect Jonathan! Joyce had all kinds of negative thoughts running through her mind. However, I was trying to think positive thoughts. It was possible that as Jonathan told us to run in one direction, he ran in the other direction to get to his house at the same time! We knew he lived in that neighborhood and was familiar with his surroundings. I told Joyce that Jonathan was going to be all right and not to worry.

Nevertheless, it was really hard to get that intimidating, shining knife out of our minds because it was the last source of threat that we saw. We hoped someone had called the police; we did not know what to think.

While I was trying to console Joyce, I continued pacing back and forth from her bedroom to the living room window to see if my parents had arrived. We were so tense and jumpy that every little sound had us running to the window. I figured I had less than 10 minutes to freshen up. And knowing my mom, she would be on time at 11:30 p.m. Mom had a signal, which was a little tap of the horn, as not to disturb others at night. So as we intently waited, I wanted to be ready to quickly walk out of the door.

As Joyce and I nervously anticipated my leaving, I stopped to give her a big, tight, cuddly hug to console her, *not knowing that would be the last time I would get to hug my close friend!* After the hug, I assured her again that Jonathan would be alright!

Then, in the stillness of the night, the faint sound of a horn caught my attention. I knew that was my mom's code—a slight tap on the horn. When I looked out the window, I saw our car. That big black Buick with wings on the tail fenders made me feel as if I was being rescued by a "Chariot with Wings!" Or you might say, in today's terms, "The Black Batmobile!" Now, I instantly felt safe and protected, just knowing my family was there.

As I opened Joyce's front door to leave, we exchanged glances, knowing the heaviness in our hearts we were both carrying. While waving good-bye, I wistfully turned and hurried down the steps to the car.

But just as my hand touched the door handle of the car, fear gripped me! "What if my sister or parents should ask me what we did or where we had gone? What am I going to say?" I thought.

My family gladly received me as I got in the car; no questions were asked.

Fortunately, they carried on with their amusing conversation, laughing and having a good time. I spoke and acted interested in what they were talking about as I tried to blend in without them detecting that there was anything wrong.

I cherished the fact that I had been rescued. I knew I was now safe and secure while sitting in the car, surrounded by my family. Family is something we all, at one time or another, take for granted. However, sometimes we all need to feel the special security of family. At Joyce's house, I felt like we had gotten away from the trouble, and I was relieved. But here in the midst of my family, I was safe, secure, loved, and protected!

EMOTIONALLY SHATTERED TO PIECES

Now the little storefront Pentecostal church was only about 3 minutes away. In spite of the short travel time, it seemed to be the longest 3 minutes of my life!!!

Things had been moving so swiftly all evening, and they were happening back-to-back!

While I was riding in the car and looking out of the window, I began to replay what had happened to me that night. I just didn't know what to do with the flood of emotions that were hitting me as my dad drove to the church. I did not realize what the terrifying and painful experience had done to me physically, emotionally, and mentally!

While all of these mixed emotions were beyond my comprehension, I pondered what I should do. I was feeling afraid, broken, nervous, rescued, relieved, and sad, and I was secretly hiding information from my family. With all these thoughts and emotions running through my mind at the same time, I was totally confused.

Normally, I could talk to my mom or my sister about most things. But in view of the fact that I had been someplace I should not have been, I didn't dare confess what had happened or try to justify why I was at that party.

Now, this was the first time I had a minute to myself to reflect on everything. I did not realize I needed time to exhale and to purge my thoughts of the devastating trauma I endured!

Suddenly, I remembered every little detail. I could still hear the ugly words that the bully had whispered in my ear. And I could still feel the physical pain I had experienced from the rough treatment of being mishandled and tossed around like a rag doll!

I recalled the embarrassment and shame I went through as people looked at me as if I had done something wrong when I was the victim.

Also, I was tormented by the questions that I had asked myself over and over again. "Why did this happen to me?" "Out of everyone in the room, why did the molester come for Flora?" "Why was I so utterly mistreated, abused, and assaulted?"

The more I thought about it, the more *I had to come to terms with the reality that I had been wounded, attacked, traumatized, broken, and crushed!* Of course, all these different and diverse emotions opened the door to all the other previous disappointments I had recently gone through! I felt completely *overwhelmed and SHATTERED!!!* *(Psalm 34:18) The Lord is close to the brokenhearted; he rescues those who are crushed in spirit.*

I was doing all I could to keep from crying, but I had to hold it in to keep anyone from knowing how I felt! This was a great amount of pressure for a 14-year-old to experience, or for anyone to experience in light of the trauma!

In those few minutes, it seemed I had lived a lifetime!

We finally made it to the church for the New Year's Eve service. My dad was trying to find a parking space near the church. Still, we ended up walking back to the church for about half a block.

As we all got out of the car and walked together, I felt a wonderful sense of unity and comfort being with my family. I needed to feel that connection.

Walking in the fresh, cool night air made a pleasant difference from being shut up in the car or in the stuffy room with Joyce and all the negative thoughts of doom and gloom!

I just wanted to forget everything that happened and try to act as normal as possible, while hoping that everything would just go away.

That night, as we approached the little storefront Pentecostal church, I looked forward to going in, and I had not felt like that in a while.

Maybe it was the excitement my mom had for this special service. She had been looking forward to this night all week with anticipation of what God was going to do. We all seemed to be in good spirits as we prepared to enter the New Year's Eve service together.

PERSONAL REFLECTIONS CONCERNING CHAPTER 2

Being broken and shattered may be a result of many events or happenings in your life, which can be very painful. Here are some thoughts to reflect on:

1. Rejection is real, and some people are trapped by it, but it is usually when you give that person or situation power over you that it may cause you to suffer. Learn how to walk in your strengths and not sit in self-pity. List your strengths:

2. When you focus on what you really want, is God in the plan at all?

3. Many times, when people are shattered or broken, they are also running from something that has hurt them extremely badly. *You must acknowledge the pain to gain the healing!* What are you running from?

4. You may be hurting now because of what has happened in your life. But always remember, there is help and there is hope! Don't stop believing in God because of a horrible experience you've endured.

5. My favorite prayer is, "Help me, Lord!"

Don't let bitterness turn you away from the main source that can help you!

Scripture Reference for the Chapter Two

All scripture is taken from the King James Version Bible unless otherwise noted.

Proverbs 19:21

You can make many plans, but the LORD's purpose will prevail. NLT

Psalm 119:146

I cried out to you; rescue me, that I may obey your laws. NLT

Psalm 34:6

In my desperation I prayed, and the Lord listened; He saved me from all my troubles. NLT

Colossians 3:20

Children, always obey your parents, for this pleases the Lord. NLT.

Psalm 34:18

The LORD is close to the brokenhearted; he rescues those who are crushed in spirit. NLT

CHAPTER THREE

THE
ULTIMATE RESCUE

THE TORMENTING MEMORY

When my family and I arrived, we entered the little storefront Pentecostal church as usual. If you have ever been in a storefront church before, you'd know the entrance was right off the sidewalk, like a regular store. Once you open the door, you're inside the rear of the church, in full view of the podium and the backs of the congregation.

However, as I entered the church that night, I expected to feel the way I normally felt. But something unusual happened.

After I crossed the threshold into the House of God, an enormous weight of guilt and shame fell on me like a ton of bricks! I felt so unworthy, so unclean, and immensely ashamed!

It had been just a few minutes ago that I had come to the knowledge of the mental and emotional trauma which I had endured. Now with this strange new feeling, I felt even more crushed, shattered, and so utterly alone and isolated!

Even though I knew I desperately needed to talk with someone, I still restrained myself. I definitely knew this was not the right time to try to talk with anyone. So, I stood in the battle alone, knowing that this was too much for me to fight by myself. I needed someone, but who could I turn to?

At that point, I was in a major dilemma as to what I should do! There was such a strong sense of confusion and helplessness bearing down on me as I tried to hold myself together!

The congregation had already started gathering around the altar, which was at the front of the church near the podium.

Now, to give you a candid look at the church, the room could probably hold about 60 people. The podium was on an elevated platform, and a curtain divided the room behind the platform for the privacy of the facilities.

Then the pastor called for everyone to come forward to join him in prayer at the altar. The goal was to have everybody in the congregation begin praying together before midnight, as the old year died out and the birth of the New Year was coming in.

As I slowly approached the altar with the others, my mind vividly took over and began reviewing the devastatingly and gross experiences that I had encountered again!

Suddenly, I felt the destructive hands of the molester touching and crawling all over my body like worms! I felt the fear afresh as I relived the horror of the dark red room! I could even feel the terror of the threat from the bully as I visualized the long knife twinkling under the streetlights. And then, it felt like the lips of the predator were pressing against my ear as he whispered ugly words that were turning over in my mind and in my stomach!

I felt extremely dirty! Underneath so much guilt and confusion, I even blamed myself for not being able to get away from that big, strong, and abusive bully!

No! No! No! I started fighting the memory and the instant replay! I did not want those ugly thoughts flooding my mind while at church. I just wanted all of the madness to go away!

Yet, it had not once occurred to me that the terrifying harassment and assault had just happened less than an hour ago! No wonder every little detail was still fresh in my mind, and I could still feel the aches and pains on my body from the roughness of being mishandled.

SOMETHING HAD TO BREAK

The pressure seemed to be mounting! I thought the others in the church would be able to tell by my countenance what I was going through. It was hard to hide the tears that slowly ran down my face. I continued to cover my face in a way to keep others from seeing it. *(Psalm 30:5) Weeping may endure for a night.*

All my hurt feelings from being on an emotional roller coaster for months surfaced in my thoughts. First, the devastation of having to move away from all that was familiar to me to a place of desolation was tearing me apart. Then the ugly, wrong choices I had made to try to fit in seemed to slap me in the face. My heartbreaking disappointments seemed to overwhelm me all at once!

My thoughts were swiftly recounting my past like a day of reckoning as I was standing there pondering these things in my heart. I felt the disenchantment and dissatisfaction with what I had been pursuing all my teen years. I had even experienced the bitter results of what I thought would bring me happiness.

First of all, the unsaved friends I wanted to be like had used me and rejected me while laughing in my face. Secondly, the friend I truly trusted betrayed me by lying to me and convincing me to lie too. It seemed as if I had been led into what felt like the pit of hell at that strange party.

Finally, the last agonizing thought I had was how I felt trapped in the dark red room as I was being attacked. The darkness was so intimidatingly frightening. I remember always having a fear of the dark since I was a small child.

While I was in a state of perplexity at the altar, I sensed such strong grief, like my little heart would burst! Being so overbearingly weighed down under such distress and pressure, I felt like I wanted to outwardly **SCREAM!!!**

So, *I consciously realized at that point that something had to break, and I didn't want it to be me!* Somehow, I knew that if I did not take power and authority over my mind in the heat of the moment, I would lose it!

As I started searching in my mind for ways to take authority over the oppressing thoughts, something came to mind. All my days of attending church and hearing the Word of God preached paid off, as a scripture came to mind: Submit *yourselves, therefore, to God.* **Resist the devil, and he will flee from you! (James 4:7)**

Oh yes, I knew I had to resist the **devil** in order to take control of my own mind. Somehow, out of nowhere, I found the strength to say "no" to the **tormenting spirit** being replayed in my mind! I was tired of being bullied, and I decided not to let them win! **The fighter in me had already perceived that the loser would be the victim of the winner! And I was determined I was not going to be the victim again!**

Although distressed, dismayed, and discontented, I knew I was in a serious battle. So I decided not to scream, or I would lose the battle. **I was in the fight of my life for my mind!**

That abusive spirit of torment is another kind of bully; it will harass, persecute, and assault you. **The unclean spirit of torment** will oppress you mentally and emotionally until you give in, give out, or give up!

I had made a strong declaration in my mind, yet I lacked the strength to push it through. I still needed some help to be free. The feeling of all those weights of guilt and shame heavily pressed me down. I felt like I was sinking and drowning under the load. I needed to be rescued, and I knew I could not rescue myself by myself.

At that moment, I realized I did not want these ugly thoughts to be my memory for the coming year or the rest of my life! I remembered saying to God, *"Lord, I don't want my past to be my future!*

HAVING A TALK WITH JESUS

Then all at once, in the chambers of my mind, I remembered my promise to God when I was in trouble at the party!

Do you remember?

I had asked God to rescue me and help me. *I said, "Lord, if you get me out of this, I will live for you!* That's when God intervened and immediately raised up Jonathan to be my hero.

Now, all of the bad stuff that constantly replayed in my mind had blocked out any good memories of that whole night. That's why the agonizing, tormenting spirit continued to work so hard to keep me from remembering my commitment to God!

Again, being at the mercy of God, I found myself

asking him to get me out of this trouble too! Fighting with the tormenting spirit had been just as scary and oppressing as the experience with the brutal, harassing bully. I brought all those heavy feelings of guilt, shame, fear, disappointment, and persecution to the Lord. Although I felt so unworthy and so disconnected from such a Holy God, I knew in my heart that He was my only hope of being free.

But in spite of my unworthiness, my shattered emotions, and my wounds, I began to repent and ask the Lord to forgive me of all my sins! I asked Him to forgive me for putting more trust in my friends than in Him. As I examined myself in His presence, all my plans and dreams that I thought were so important now seemed like dung or manure! *(Acts 3:19) Repent ye therefore, and be converted, that your sins may be blotted out…*

I cried out, **"Save me, Jesus; save me, Lord!"**

Those were the words flowing from my mouth. This time, they were *my words*, not the words of someone who told me to repeat after them. *(Psalm 55:16) As for me, I will call upon God, and the LORD shall save me.*

This time, I knew I needed Jesus to rescue me; He was the only one who could! I remember calling on Jesus and asking Him to save me and deliver me from the tight grip of sin that the devil had on me like Jaws!

As I cried out for help at the altar, I could hear myself saying, "Help me, Lord!" But on the inside, I was screaming out for help much louder! Because by now I could feel myself sinking or drowning swiftly from the heaviness that was pressing down on me like an anvil on my back! My sincere prayer from the heart was, Help, Lord, please rescue me! Lord, set me free from these awful feelings of being wounded, broken, and shattered to pieces! Help me, Jesus; don't let me lose my mind, and don't let me go out like this! *(Psalm 147:3) He heals the brokenhearted and binds up their wounds.*

Suddenly, I realized I had actually talked to Jesus and told Him all my troubles. I had poured out everything before Him while desperately standing at the altar in His presence!

Do you remember earlier when I said I needed to talk to someone? Well, I found that someone to be **Jesus!** The more I talked to Jesus, the more involved I became in my conversation as well as in my surrender to Him. The only thing that had my attention at this point was getting help from the only source that I knew who had the power to help me! **JESUS!**

I recalled that it was in this church that I had learned to sing about Jesus. I had felt His presence, and I rejoiced in this room many times. I had memorized scriptures from Sunday school and won the prizes nearly every Sunday for the student who knew the Word of God. I could remember a lot of good things happening in this church and the feelings of contentment I usually had while standing at the altar, but this time things were different! This time, I was desperate for healing, deliverance, and change. And I was determined not to leave this place the same way I came!

(Psalm 34:18) The LORD is close to the brokenhearted; He rescues those who are crushed in spirit.

THE VISION:
THE FIGHT OF MY LIFE, FOR MY LIFE

After my desperate talk with Jesus, things were changing. Now in *my spirit,* I could hear the voice of Jesus saying, *"Come to me; I am your help!"*

But in *my mind's eye,* I could see and feel myself sinking into this deep, dark, marshy pit that appeared out of nowhere, which reminded me of quicksand.

Let me describe the reality of *the Marshy Pit* to you. It seemed to be a very large body of deep, slimy, thick mud. The space around me was empty, with a creepy, dismal feeling of being totally alone. The smell was that of rotten eggs and animal dung, which I seemed to breathe in with every breath. Somehow I was planted in this muddy, stinky place, like a stick in the mud.

Nevertheless, I had a feeling I was near the shore, which made me think that if I struggled more to get out, I could manage to reach the shore. Unfortunately, the more I struggled, the deeper I was sinking. I felt utterly trapped! There was no one around to turn to for help. While feeling extremely tired and overwhelmed by my fight to be free, I continued to call on Jesus to please help me!

I was trying to reach up for Jesus to pull me out of this horrible pit. Nevertheless, with all of my attempts to get out of this murky pit, going down seemed to be unavoidable. The mud was like a vacuum. The more I tried to get out, the more I was being suctioned into the depths of this miry clay or swamp. Yet I did not give up for fear that the muddy quicksand would soon overtake me and I would completely drown!

Despite, being so confused, I asked myself, *"Why is*

all of this happening to me?"

Somehow, the question troubled my thoughts, even while I was stuck in the dark, marshy pit. Why? This is a question every broken or shattered person will ask themselves, as if there is a satisfactory answer to the question.

While the darkness around me felt as thick as the mud, I could not see anything. I sensed the eerie presence of fear, my own frailty, and weakness. As I was straining to see through the darkness, trying to find any hope of help, I could only perceive the strange isolation of loneliness. I even wondered in my mind if I was in hell!

Yet, *I continued to pray* in that dark, dreadful place. I assured God that what I had left behind that night was not the life I wanted to pursue! So I presented myself to God afresh, asking Him to give me new thoughts and desires. I knew I wanted to live a saved life—to feel free, clean, and brand new!

I asked God to please give me a mind and a will to serve Him all the days of my life!

Without a doubt, I then realized that was not a simple prayer of repentance but a sincere prayer of commitment! *I had committed my life to God! (Psalm 37:5) Commit thy way unto the LORD; trust also in him, and he shall bring it to pass.*

Somehow, I knew in my heart that He would rescue me, even though I was slowly sinking into what seemed like a bottomless pit. I disregarded the overshadowing of the darkness and continued to pray.

Suddenly, my eyes picked up a tiny light in the distance. I could see the small light appear out of nowhere. The size of the light was like a pinhead, and it was moving slowly towards me. The light let me know that someone was there! Hope filled my heart as I anticipated that help was on the way!

LOVE PULLED ME OUT OF A HORRIBLE PIT

I began to cry out as loud as I could! I said, "Help me! Please get me out of this mess!" was my plea!

The more I hollered out for help, the more the filthy mud from the marsh was getting into my mouth. At this point, the muddy substance was all over me, and I was sinking up to my neck as I felt the weight of the marsh pulling me down even more.

Then, like a smooth, soft, gentle wind, I could barely hear a faint, small, sweet voice calling and saying, "***Come to me!***"

And in the midst of all the darkness and eeriness, I began to feel a tranquil peace come over me! This time, instead of fighting and struggling to get out, I had learned not to panic. I reached up with all my might toward the light as I saw it come down from above. The presence of the light brought a pleasant peacefulness, and I was no longer afraid of the terrifying dark marsh. That wonderful, small ray of light subdued the intimidating darkness as I focused on it.

However, I kept trying to reach up in hopes that someone would come to my rescue. I noticed that my hands and arms were now totally extended above the mud. I felt some degree of change. Now I could sense that someone was there. But it seemed to be a test of my faith or endurance as to why I was not lifted out of the marshy pit right away.

Then I noticed that my words were the powerful motivating factor behind my deliverance. As I would say, *"Save me, Jesus!"* I noticed I was being loosened from the suction and the tightness of the mud. So, I continued to plead, **"Save me, Jesus!"**

I could tell the Lord heard me! I felt a slight motion and movement around me in the darkness. Then, I felt myself being slowly lifted up from the horrible miry clay as I called on Jesus to save me. Finally, I realized I was being drawn up and out of the awful, muddy, stinky, dark, and dreadful pit! ***The Lord simply pulled me out of that terrifying place!*** I did not see it happening, but I felt myself moving upward from the tight grip of the thick quicksand. Finally, before I knew it, I was standing on top of the deep, murky mud. And I was not sinking anymore. It happened so quickly that I was still in awe of how smoothly the transition took place.

OMG! I had a victorious awakening when I realized that ***the thing which once held me captive was now under my feet!***

I frantically rejoiced at being so miraculously set free from the prison of damnation! I rejoiced with ultimate gratitude as I repeatedly said, **"Thank you, Jesus!!!"**

FOLLOW THE SOUND OF HIS VOICE

Although I was freed from the tight grip of the dark, marshy pit that held me down, I was still in a place of darkness. It seemed as if my transition was progressing in stages. Yes, I was now standing on top of the marsh, but darkness was still a major factor. Even though I was able to see a little from the small ray of light, my eyes could only see what was close around me.

Then I noticed that every time I asked Jesus to save me or to help me, He would say, "Come to me!"

Again, I cried out for help! I needed the Lord to completely deliver me from the present dismal place of darkness. Just as I was about to cry out again, the small, sweet, gentle voice that I heard before said, "Come to me!"

But this time, the voice was behind me in the distance. For some reason, things had changed that quickly, so I felt compelled to answer the loving command by saying, "Yes, Lord!" I then turned around to follow the sound of the voice, and *a whole new world opened up before my eyes!*

While I was standing on the top of the marsh, I was still in deep darkness, but when I turned around to follow the voice of Jesus, I turned to total brightness, and there was no darkness anywhere. To my amazement, all of the darkness was totally gone! Praise the Lord!

What a distinctive change from extreme darkness to extreme light! Wow! I was literally blinded! The bright, beautiful light that was before my eyes was too awesome for words!

THE LORD HAD BROUGHT ME OUT OF DARKNESS INTO HIS MARVELOUS LIGHT!

(John 8:12) Jesus said, "I am the light of the world; he that follows me shall not walk in darkness but shall have the light of life."

After turning to the light, I began to walk toward the voice, and suddenly I was completely out of the muddy pit and out of the darkness too! You see, I noticed that the Lord was continuously answering my prayers as I asked Him!

I knew it was through His magnificent love that I was rescued, set free, and delivered. Now, I confidently felt helped by the strong, powerful love and mercy that swept over my soul in the presence of the Lord!

The excitement of being freed from the horrible things I overcame—I just could not imagine feeling anything better or greater than at that moment! I was so overjoyed and excited about my victory that I just wanted to continue to rejoice!

Although I was glad to be out of the terrifying abyss, I was still completely covered from my head to my toes by the smelly, muddy clay. Immediately, the clay started drying and getting hard all over my body.

HEALING HANDS OF LOVE

Then I prayed and asked Jesus to *"clean up my body from the stinky mud and make me brand new!"* This was another prayer request I had placed before Him.

Instantly, without a word, I saw two of the most beautiful, brightly illuminated hands come down from above!

Remember, I had been traumatized by *destructive hands that assaulted and abused me,* but now I was being saved by these *huge*, *glorious, Loving Hands that came to rescue me*! As the love of God strongly surrounded me, I could feel the hands of God securely protecting me!

Now I was thoroughly confident that since Jesus had answered my previous prayers, He would not leave me dirty or unclean with dried mud and clay all over my body.

Therefore, I began to rejoice! The more I rejoiced, jumping and dancing in His awesome presence, the more the ugly, muddy clay started falling off of me. Now, I had the *freedom to move,* which intensified my rejoicing even more!

While I was rejoicing, those powerful, illuminated

Loving Hands seemed to generate healing rays all over my dirty, unclean, and undone body. Instantly, I started feeling better, and I did not want that glorious, soothing feeling to end.

I continued to rejoice by repeatedly saying, **"Thank you, Jesus!"**

As I bountifully gave thanksgiving, I noticed that I was no longer muddy and no longer dirty. Even the disgusting stench from the pit was gone from my body. I felt **F-R-E-E**, and I felt **C-L-E-A-N!!!**

Praise the Lord! A miracle had taken place! I never saw the wonderful **Loving Hands** of healing touch me, but somehow I knew they did! *I sensed it was His love, grace, and mercy that pulled me out* of the horrible pit of death and destruction! And I knew it was a *Miracle of Love* that cleansed me from all my sins and healed my body. I felt like a new person!

(Psalm 40:2) He brought me up also out of a horrible pit, out of the miry clay, and set my feet upon a rock, and established my goings.

HIS LOVE WAS CALLING TO ME

As I was standing in awe of His mighty presence, *love was continuously overflowing in my heart as I*

79

praised the Lord for answered prayers! Then, in the midst of all my joy and gladness, I still heard the sweet, calming voice of Jesus say, "Come to me!" So I quieted my rejoicing to hear what the Lord was saying.

Again, I heard the soft, mellow tone of His voice say, "Come to me!" And my reply was, "Yes, Lord!" However, I then realized God was not finished with me yet! In my heart, it seemed important to the Lord that I knew He was with me all the time!

Next, the Lord revealed to me how *His Hand* was on our lives—me, Joyce, and Jonathan as well. He showed me how he rescued us that night, even though we were not aware of it. Yes, Jesus was there at the party when the attacker put his destructive hands on me. Jesus was there when Jonathan (my hero) boldly spoke up on my behalf. Jesus was there when we were threatened and terrorized at the sight of the knife in the hands of the bully. And as the gang gathered at each end of the alley to block us, Jesus was there!

He even gave Jonathan the plan to save our lives. He was with us as we ran across the busy, four-lane street without ever stopping!

What an awesome, jaw-dropping revelation for me

to receive! Jesus let me know He was with me all the time!

I was filled with amazement to know that He cared for me so much and that I was never completely alone. I began to weep as I felt so overwhelmed by His continuous and unconditional love for me.

Remember? I was the one running from the Lord, but He was right there all the time. *He let me know, in spite of my behavior, that He knew the sincerity of my heart.*

The Lord saw something in me that I did not see in myself. He knew, deep down within me, that I wanted a better life than the one I was pursuing. So the Lord pressed me to make a choice. Even though I was afraid of many things that happened at the party that night, in my heart, I decided to make Jesus my choice!

It seemed He loved me enough to pick me out—to be picked on! It was very hard for me to comprehend that I was even worth the trouble. I could barely grasp the magnitude of such *love overflowing in my heart and mind!*

Then I heard the voice of the Lord lovingly say to me again, "Come to me." And I willingly replied, "Yes, Lord!"

It seemed as if He was preparing me for something as He spoke calming *Words of Life into my spirit.*

"Yes, Lord," continued coming out of my mouth. I was so captivated by His *Words of Life* that seemed to be healing my spirit.

As I listened, the Lord answered the question of why He allowed these things to happen, and the answer was absolutely plain. The Lord said, *"Because I have chosen you!"*

Immediately, I bowed down as I surrendered myself in His awesome presence. I pondered, "The Lord had chosen me. I could not even imagine that He saw something in me that He could use for His glory." I was humbled by the thought that God desired to use me.

I asked, "What do you see in me, Lord?"

The Lord spoke of qualities and characteristics that He pointed out in me; He saw my heart, and in spite of my natural actions, deeply within me I had a true heart after God. When the going got tough, my surrender to Him was genuine as I humbled myself in His presence.

Secondly, I had learned to listen and hear His voice. And I willingly obeyed as I said, "Yes, Lord," in response to the commands that were given to me. Lastly, the Lord showed me the powerful fighter and warrior in me that was determined not to fail or give up in spite of what I had faced. In the midst of every test I endured, I had risen to victory in every stage that He had taken me through.

With every **Word of Life** He spoke to me, I treasured those words in my heart. And I knew there was something greater in store for me! I started praising God like I had won a billion dollars! *I felt Super-Special!!!*

I noticed that all the different stages that the Lord had taken me through seemed to escalate with greater Glory, Power, and Love!

At each stage, I didn't think the glory of God could be any more powerful or greater than it was at that moment!

But I was so wrong! It seemed that with every stage, the love of Jesus was more infused and supercharged inside of me. I just didn't want to leave His awesome presence at any of the stages because they were all absolutely divine.

What I did not know was that after all the wonderful, great, and mighty things God had already done for me… *The Best Was Yet to Come!*

PERSONAL REFLECTIONS CONCERNING CHAPTER 3

Truly, the struggle is real when you are trying to break free from something that has a stronghold on you. But in Chapter 3, we see there is hope and there is help!

1. Name the thing(s) you are struggling with that seem to control your mind.

2. You *must* face the tormenting spirit in order to take dominion over it. I learned that if you don't *face it*, you can't *dominate it.*

3. Do you really know where your help comes from? It's never too late to turn to Jesus. His Loving Hands are outstretched to you even now!

4. God has a magnificent plan for your life, and sometimes things happen so you can make a conscious decision to follow Him!

5. God is looking for you to say, **"Yes, Lord, I surrender all to you!"**

All scripture is taken from the King James Version
Bible unless otherwise noted.

Psalm 30:5
For his anger is but for a moment; his favor is for
life: weeping may endure for a night, but joy comes
in the morning. NKJV

James 4:7
Submit yourselves therefore to God. Resist the
devil, and he will flee from you.

Acts 3:19
Repent ye, therefore, and be converted, that your
sins may be blotted out…

Psalm 55:16
As for me, I will call upon God, and the LORD
shall save me. NKJV

Psalm 147:3
He heals the brokenhearted, and binds up their
wounds. NKJV

Psalm 34:18
The LORD is close to the brokenhearted; he rescues
those who are crushed in spirit. NLT

Psalm 37:5

Commit thy way unto the LORD; trust also in him; and he shall bring it to pass.

John 8:12

Then Jesus spoke to them again, saying, I am the light of the world: he who follows me shall not walk in darkness, but have the light of life. NKJV

Psalm 40:2

He brought me up also out of a horrible pit, out of the miry clay, and set my feet upon a rock, and established my goings.

LOVE BROUGHT ME OUT

Love pulled me out of the "Miry Clay,"
Love rescued me and forgave me of my sins that day.

Love stretched out His hands and touched my soul,
Love Himself made me clean and whole.

Love wooed me with His calm and comforting voice,
Love gave me hope and peace that I may reach up and rejoice.

Love's intense fire purged me through and through,

Love's glorious presence fashioned me and made me "Brand New."

Love himself was drawing me by Personal Invitation,

Love said "Come," and I said "Yes" to Divine Transformation!

By: Flora L. Jackson

CHAPTER FOUR

FASHIONED BY LOVE

ONE MOMENT IN TIME FOREVER CHANGED MY LIFE!

All of a sudden, I realized that God was not through with me yet!

Then I heard that same awesome, sweet, loving voice say, *"Flora, look up!"*

All the other times, the Lord simply said, "Come to me," but this time He called me by my name. I knew there was something different about to happen. *Because when He called my name, I felt a shift in the atmosphere.* He called my name with purpose, and there was a greater elevation of God's Glory, which filled the atmosphere immediately!

However, this next stage took me by complete surprise!

I will try to describe the Powerful Glory that my eyes beheld at that moment. But I will tell you that my description is void of the extraordinary power which I experienced, *for this was the moment that ultimately changed my life, for the rest of my life!*

After I followed the command from the voice and looked up, I was absolutely amazed at what I saw!

Suddenly the sky opened up, and there was a huge white cloud over my head. The cloud was actively rolling as if something spectacular was about to happen! Again, I saw the two powerful **Loving Hands of the Lord** coming down from heaven, even closer to me this time. These extraordinary, radiant hands were so blindingly illuminating that they seemed to flash huge beams of light like enormous diamond clusters! And the spectacular fire that surrounded the glorious hands glistened like the purest gold!

I don't know how my natural eyes stood the magnificence and the brilliant magnitude of this Supernatural display, which was totally astonishing and breathtaking! *I felt so small underneath this artistry of God's Glorious, Loving Power!* The mighty Glory of God and the Love of God were so encompassing. The presence of the Lord seemed so overpowering as the bright, golden glow and shimmering colors of the rainbow reflected off of His Beautiful Hands! I didn't know if my eyes, heart, and body could take such radiance, but I could not look away!!!

Then, as if this was not enough, something else happened. The rolling white cloud opened up, and in the center of that cloud was a brilliantly illuminated **Fiery Ladder!** As it began to slowly come down from heaven, it was just too much for my eyes to focus upon. OMG! What awesome beauty for me to behold! I was absolutely speechless and captivated by this phenomenal, wonderful and amazing happening!

I thought I had already experienced the power of God when He set me free from sin and then cleansed my body! At that time, there was so much love, joy, and freedom that I could not imagine anything greater! It had already been an awesome, joyful journey of one victory after another!

But this! This was something so spectacular that I truly thought the beauty alone would cause me to die and go to heaven at that exact moment!

Feeling so unworthy to be in this breathtaking atmosphere, I fell to my knees at the Power and Glory of God that surrounded me as I humbled myself in His Presence and surrendered to *His*

Majestic Love!

THE SUPERNATURAL GLORY OF GOD WAS EVERYWHERE

My little heart was saturated with the newness of this overwhelming level of *Love and Glory* that filled my whole body, soul, and spirit! I thought a portion of heaven had come down, for the Glory of the Lord was everywhere. As far as I could see, there was the manifested Glory of God! What could I compare this stupendous event to? It was like I had a *personal revival* in paradise come down from heaven, just for me!

Then, from this spectacular scene, the illuminating Fiery Ladder came closer and closer until it touched the ground. There was not a hint of darkness anywhere. The fire seemed to be a blazing, golden color with huge rays of glittering sparkles. And the awesome brilliance of the light covered every step and every side of the magnificent Fiery Ladder!

As I stood in front of the penetrating beam of *Pure Light*, I could see that I was not all clean! I thought, "Oh, no! I still had some dirty spots, and my mouth still has mud in it!" I began to cry out to God again! I said, "Lord, please make me completely clean; I don't want to be partially clean. I want to be made whole and made Brand New in your presence, right now!"

(Psalm 139:23-24) Search me, O God, and know my heart; test me and know my thoughts. Point out anything in me that offends you; and lead me along the path of everlasting life.

As my prayer request was released in such a powerful **atmosphere of flaming fire**, it appeared that little fire bolts started jumping off the Fiery Ladder into my small body. Wow! Although I was not as close as I wanted to be to the ladder, I felt the extreme heat penetrating through me! Yet I was not burned up, but the fire appeared to be burning off the dirty stuff that was hiding in the crevices of my body!

I even leaned forward so God could get all the mud and the dirty stuff off of me. I just wanted Him to do whatever He wanted to do, as I yielded to Him. I sensed that I was being cleansed in a bath of fire, but how refreshing the flames of fire felt in His awesome presence!

AN INVITATION TO GREATNESS

Immediately, I knew I was being changed into something valuable and useful for the Glory of God! After all this happened, I heard the Lord say, **"Flora, come up to me!"** There was a change in the soft, sweet, gentle instructions. This time, His voice was stronger and more compelling.

This no longer appeared to be a rescue mission; this was now a firm command or an Entreating Invitation to Greatness!

I perceived with this command that the voice was telling me to come up the extremely hot, burning ladder.

Oh my God! I felt a small amount of fear overtake me for a moment as I assessed my hands touching the blazing hot fire on the ladder! There was such an awesome greatness of power surrounding me that I felt too inadequate to try to climb up the majestic Fiery Ladder by myself.

Yet I wanted to obey the voice of the Lord, so I timidly answered with, "Yes, Lord."

I started walking toward the ladder, but it was not as close as I thought it was. So I then started running to the ladder with all my might. I finally reached the foot of the mighty golden Fiery Ladder. The radiance was blazingly blinding, and the heat was extremely intense, but my desire to get up the ladder became more intense! I knew I had to do it!

I continued to say, "Yes, Lord" in my heart as I

reached for the ladder. Then I tried to pull myself up, but I could not get my foot up to the first step. Why? I was so ready to get up this ladder. I pressed forward in spite of my fear, and failed.

I was very disappointed, yet I tried it again. This time I grabbed the sides of the ladder with all my strength and tried to pull myself up, but I failed again. And then I tried it a third time, but no matter how hard I tried, I could not pull myself up. I was just too heavy for my own strength.

I thought, "What's weighing me down?" I fell down on my back from the weight that seemed to be pulling me backwards. I just laid there looking up to the radiant, sparkling, beautiful Healing Hands that had been there for me the whole time. Yet I did not know what to do to accomplish my goal.

Confused and disappointed, I was trying to figure out what I should do.

Then I heard the Lord's strong and commanding voice say to me, *"Flora, get up! Shake off the heavy load, and come up to me!"*

Although I did not know what the problem was, I trusted God. Immediately, a great boldness and strength stood up inside of me as I quickly got up off the ground!

That's when I discovered that I was carrying a heavy load on my back. It seemed to be like an almost invisible lead vest or hoodie, but only under God's intense light was it revealed! No wonder I felt so heavy and could not even get up the bottom step of the ladder.

But what was it that ultimately hindered me from reaching my goal? What was trying to stop me? What was the heavy load that I carried? I had come too far to give up now! I desperately called out to the Lord for help once again! I poured out my heart to Him and declared that I was not going to give up or let anything keep me from getting up the ladder to reach my goal!

The Lord revealed to me that it was the *heavy spirit of torment* that was trying to attach itself to me by hiding as an invisible, heavy garment on my back.

Oh yes! I vividly recalled the hard battle I had fought for my mind and for my life. However, in the brilliant, Fiery Light of God's Glory, nothing unclean could hide without it being exposed or uncovered!

You cannot imagine the awesome power and authority I felt come over me! I realized that God had already given me strength to overcome the ugly, tormenting spirit which once oppressed me so heavily that I wanted to **scream!**

But wait a minute! *I remembered that I had already taken authority over that unclean spirit of torment, and I won!* The devil must be crazy to try to make me think I was not free when *I had already won that battle! My Victory Was Sealed!*

Now, all I had to do was simply obey the voice of the Lord and get up, shake it off, and come up to Him as instructed! My heart leaped with joy, and I knew in my spirit that this *Victory Was Already Mine!!!*

Quickly, *I got up* from the ground, and like an experienced fighter, I was determined to knock out the opponent without any apprehensions! Being filled with new strength and power, *I shook off* with little effort the heavy load that was trying to hold me down! *(John 8:36) So if the Son sets you free, you will be free indeed.*

Immediately, *I started running to the Lord,* as He had commanded me to do! I ran with all my might, as if I were running for my life, to the blazing, golden Fiery Ladder!

Hallelujah! **I was praising God for my Victory before I got to my Destiny!!!**

TRANSFORMED BY: THE HOLY SPIRIT & MADE BRAND NEW

By the time I got close enough to the ladder, I just leaped in the air! Gravity could not hold me down. I had no weights, no mud, and no fear; this time there were no barriers between my soul and my Savior. As I leaped, it felt like I was flying, and as soon as my foot touched the bottom step, I swiftly pulled myself up onto the magnificent, illuminating Fiery Ladder!

Suddenly, I felt a great and powerful jolt hit me from the crown of my head to the soles of my feet, like a lightning bolt! And my mouth was instantly filled with heavenly language! I began to speak in other tongues, which is the manifestation of the Holy Spirit or Holy Ghost! (Acts 2:4) And they were all filled with the Holy Spirit and began to speak with other tongues as the Spirit gave them utterance.

Oh my God! I had never felt so fulfilled in all of my life! I felt the power of God's Love overshadowing my body completely! This was not about *a mere feeling of love;* this was about a **genuine** *happening of Love! Love Himself had changed me!* I knew that I was *instantly transformed* inside and out!

Without a doubt, I knew I was Saved, Sanctified, and filled with the Mighty Power of the Holy Spirit, and I was fully made Brand New!

(Ephesians 2:9-10) For, we are God's masterpiece. He has created us anew in Christ Jesus, so that we can do the good things he planned for us long ago.

Whatever the Lord did in the different stages of my supernatural vision seemed to crescendo or build up to this supernatural, magnificent stage! Glory to his precious name! This experience was too precious to leave without getting all that God had for me! So, I just lingered in His presence.

My insatiable hunger for more overwhelmed me. I wanted more and more of the glorious fire and power that was burning within my soul. Then, I reached up with a new determination to go higher up the extraordinary Fiery Ladder!

I could hear the Lord say, "Will you love me and serve me all the days of your life?" My reply was, "Yes, Lord!"

Then He asked me, "Can I trust you to obey me and carry my Word to others?" Again, my reply was, "Yes, Lord!"

However, this was more than just saying, "Yes,

Lord," this was a response to a Loving Savior, asking for my commitment to an *"Invitation to Greatness!"* My *"Yes, Lord," was my willingness to fulfill the God-Given assignment.*

At that point, I knew the Lord had just equipped, entrusted, and empowered me to fulfill whatever the assignment was that He had for me! I felt as if I was being elevated from an earthly realm to a heavenly realm!

It is still so hard to explain, yet it's so rewarding to have experienced this phenomenal journey!

With great expectation, my hands and arms were fully extended as I was climbing and pulling myself up the blazing Fiery Ladder, continuously working my way up to the next level.

The supernatural, glorious fires jolted repeatedly into my small body. It was like powerful electrical currents were flowing through every area of my being!

Now, getting to the next step on the ladder was my main and ultimate goal. It seemed as if I was about to touch the powerful Loving Hands of Jesus, which were still extended to me. Oh My God! The closer I got to His Awesome Hands, the greater the brightness and the heat intensified. **My anticipation**

was on 10!

I was extremely focused on His Hands reaching out to me. His love was still compelling me to come up higher! Again, I felt the intense *"Invitation to Greatness"* flowing from His Powerful Loving Hands! I was determined more than ever to reach up and touch Him!.

I could only imagine what it would be like to touch Him. Just touching the blazing Fiery Ladder sent jolts of power through my body, but what would actually happen if I touched the Hands of the Lord?

The Holy Spirit had me so caught up as I was spiritually lifted and elevated into a heavenly dimension. All I could see was God's Glory, and all I could feel was His Supernatural Presence! His awesome power, joy, peace, goodness, and His amazing love were overflowing inside of me like a *Supernatural Revival!!!*

"Yes, Lord!" rang out of my mouth from the depths of my heart and soul!

I anxiously anticipated a great and powerful connection! *In my mind's eye, I could see my hand and His Hand come together with a supernatural explosion as they touched!* I could already feel the connection happening in my spirit. Now my absolute, ultimate goal seemed to be within my immediate reach!

As I praised the Lord with anticipation, I extended my outstretched hand with all my might. In my heart, I was saying, "Yes, Lord!" Yet, with my mouth, I was speaking in a heavenly language. With my arm lifted up as high as I could reach, I continued reaching and reaching!

At that moment, I greatly anticipated a miraculous touch from the Hand of Jesus. Nevertheless, I sensed a different touch instead!

THEN, ALL OF A SUDDEN, SOMETHING UNEXPECTED HAPPENED!

It was not the same touch as what I was experiencing at the time. No, this was different. I realized this was a normal, natural touch. This was the touch of my mother's hand. In reality, *my mother had grabbed my hand as I was reaching up for Jesus' Powerful Hand, as in my vision!*

Suddenly, I could hear a host of voices around me, praising God! That's when I realized I was no longer alone. Then I heard my mother's voice as she asked me if I was ready to get up from the floor. Since I was still caught up in the spirit, my reply was still, "Yes, Lord!"

What Happened? Well, I believe that while I was focused on a greater spiritual touch, that I was interrupted by a natural human touch!

God knows that as much as I love my mother, no human touch could ever compare with the miraculous touch that I was experiencing.

Still I continued to say, "Yes, Lord," but it seemed that my awesome Intimate Transforming Vision had just come to an end.

JESUS I WILL NEVER FORGET

Oh, how I wanted to finish my extraordinary encounter with my precious Lord and Savior, Jesus Christ. I joyously saw myself climbing that awesome, glorious, Fiery Ladder, reaching up to touch Jesus' Loving and Powerful Hands.

However, I knew in my heart that I had already reached the Lord! I never saw His Beautiful, Healing and Loving Hands touch my hand in my vision, but somehow I knew **HE HAD TOUCHED ME!**

Although His presence was overflowing in my natural body, I knew He had given me a Brand New Spiritual Body, Mind, Soul, and Spirit, as in my vision!

*(2 Corinthians 5:17-18) This means that anyone who belongs to Christ has become a new person. The old life is gone; a new life has begun! 18) And all of this is a gift from God...***PRAISE THE LORD!**

There is no amount of superlatives to describe the grandeur of HIS Glory! All I can say is that it was the most beautiful, LIFE-CHANGING experience of my life!!!

I was ***transformed*** from a sinner to a Born-Again Child of God! And I was made Brand New inside and out, right then and there in God's Glorious Presence! I was Saved, Set Free, Delivered, and Filled with Jesus' Love and the Fiery Power of the Holy Spirit!

My mother used to sing a song often around the house that says, ***"Jesus, I'll Never Forget What You've Done for Me. Jesus, I'll Never Forget How You Set Me Free!"*** Now I can sing that song with new joy and meaning. For truly, what God did for me, to me, and through me will never be forgotten! I will never forget how ***His extraordinary love brought me from Shattered glass to a beautifully sculptured, fashioned diamond!***

Even though I was no longer caught up in my vision, I could still feel that powerful heat and love penetrating through my body. I knew that I was not the same, and I knew that everything about me had changed!

What the devil had meant for bad that New Year's Eve, God turned things around for my good! Praise the Lord! Instead of running from God, I ran right into His arms, and His Loving Hands rescued me! *(Acts 3:19)Repent ye therefore, and be converted, that your sins may be blotted out, when the times of refreshing shall come from the presence of the Lord.*

When New Year's Day came in as a newborn baby, *so did I.* **I was a Brand New baby in Jesus Christ!**

Yes! It Was That Moment That Ultimately Changed My Life For The Rest Of My Life!!!

I wrote a song later in my life that described my encounter with the enemy that New Year's Eve night. The words say:

"GOD TURNED IT AROUND, HE TURNED IT AROUND!
THE WORKS OF THE ENEMY, THE SNARE SET FOR ME, BECAME THE ENEMIES DEFEAT WHEN GOD TURNED; HE TURNED, IT AROUND!"

PERSONAL REFLECTIONS CONCERNING CHAPTER 4

If you have had a spiritual encounter with God, do not take it for granted. Go back in your mind and remember, recall, and refresh what it was like.

1. Can you imagine how much God loves you?

2. His love is so personal; He has a customized story just for you in His presence.

3. Write out the highlights you remember from your personal encounter with the Lord. It's your testimony and it's your transformation story!

4. Don't let the enemy (the devil) make you think that you are not free when he knows you have the victory over your past sins and hurts. Stand on your victory!

5. Being made 'Brand New' is just a matter of saying, Yes, Lord," with all your heart!

6. If you have been changed, converted, born again, or made a brand new creation, then you have been "Fashioned by His Love." He deserves the Praise, the Honor, and the Glory! You cannot praise God too much!

All scripture is taken from the King James Version
Bible unless otherwise noted.

Psalm 139:23-24
Search me, O God, and know my heart; test me and
know my thoughts. Point out anything in me that
offends you; and lead me along the path of
everlasting life. NLT

John 8:36
So if the Son sets you free, you will be free indeed.
NIV

Acts 2:4
And they were all filled with the Holy Spirit and
began to speak with other tongues, as the Spirit
gave them utterance. NKJV

Ephesians 2:10
For, we are God's masterpiece. He has created us
anew in Christ Jesus, so we can do the good things
he planned for us long ago. NLT

2 Corinthians 5:17-18
This means that anyone who belongs to Christ has
become a new person. The old life is gone; a new
life has begun! 18) And all of this is a gift from
God… How beautiful is that? NLT

Acts 3:19

Repent ye therefore, and be converted, that your sins may be blotted out, when the times of refreshing shall come from the presence of the Lord.

CHAPTER FIVE

CHANGED INTO A
PRECIOUS DIAMOND

TIME HAS NO LIMIT IN GOD'S PRESENCE

After I realized that all of this was a vision and
that I was now back to myself, I thought I had been
*standing in prayer at the altar for just a few
minutes*. But in reality, my mother said **the time
frame had actually taken over 2 hours.** Of course,
it was as if we were in two different places at the
same time. Mom tells the story from her point of
view. And she describes her account of what
happened after I went to the altar that night.
Remember, we were there praying the old year out
and the New Year in?

My mother shared that she had been a little
concerned about me because I had been so quiet in
the car that night after leaving my friend Joyce's
house. However, she decided not to bother me since

it was so close to prayer time. Her eyes were on me as I was standing in prayer with the congregation. Then suddenly, she saw me drop to my knees with my hands raised to heaven as a sign of surrender to the Lord. But then I fell forward from my knees, face down, onto the floor, speaking in unknown tongues, or **Heavenly Language, which is the manifestation of the Holy Spirit!**

At that point, the whole congregation went into a roaring praise as they all witnessed me being filled with the Holy Spirit.

My mother said, "We praised God with you as long as we could. But you kept being energized and recharged, so we decided to leave you alone with God." The whole service continued as I actively participated in my vision while on the floor.

Mom also said, "We could all tell that you were not with us even though you were in the same room, but that you were caught away in the Spirit with the Lord!" She commented on how the Pastor even made remarks about what a glorious time I must be having with the Lord in the Spirit as he continued preaching his sermon that night.

Mom said, *"I knew you were never going to be the same again!"* She described, that there were times I would rise up like I was reaching up, and then fall back down and reach up again! As my mother was intently watching me, she knew I was totally unaware of anything going on around me in the same room of the sanctuary.

No matter what was happening in the service, she said, I continued untiringly to speak in Heavenly Language. And then, at times, there were continuous series of me saying, "Yes, Lord!"

I remember when I came out of the miraculous vision, I was saying, "Yes, Lord!" Then I plainly heard my mom's voice saying, "Praise Him, Baby; tell the Lord, yes!" Without hesitation, she wrapped me tightly in her arms while she was praising God and rejoicing along with me!

I remember being so full of the Holy Spirit and fire that I just wanted to stand up and shout out loud glorious praises to the Lord!

However, as I tried to stand, my legs were weak and wobbly, as if I had been climbing stairs or running a marathon in real life. Finally, I managed to stand, and I threw my hands up with a thunderous praise to God!

Before I knew it, my dad, who played the drums for the church, had jumped up from behind the drums and began to run around the church weeping. He started speaking in Heavenly Language, and rejoicing in the Lord! I never saw my dad so moved by the Holy Spirit before in my life.

Suddenly, my sister Jerry and I seemed to have exchanged places! For as soon as they picked me up off the floor, the next thing I knew, my sister was slain in the Spirit on the floor! Jerry was crying out to God and speaking in Heavenly tongues as she was touched by the Holy Spirit!

My! My! My! How greatly the presence of the Lord moved upon us. The people in the congregation were rejoicing and praising God for the miracles that had taken place in their lives during the service that night, too! Victoriously, the people were testifying about the changes, conversions, deliverances, and healings that happened to them all over the room, and no one seemed to be left out! What a Wonderful Lord to include everyone who would worship Him in the Spirit! *(Ps 16:11) In thy presence is fullness of joy; at thy right hand there are pleasures for evermore.*

The Holy Ghost fires that rested upon us in the service reminded me of the Mighty, Powerful Rays of the Glory of God that had penetrated my very being in the vision!

However, the Lord not only touched me; He

touched everyone praising and reaching up to Him in the room. What a wonderful, overwhelming, and glorious manifestation of the presence of the Lord! Truly, our hearts did burn with such an outpouring of miracles and blessings!

That little storefront Pentecostal church at 59th and Halsted in Chicago, Illinois, was on fire with the glory of the Lord during that special New Year's Day Service!

The Holy Spirit transformed my family. What God did for us made such a big difference in our lives and our home that we were never the same again!

Those magnificent, unusual 2 hours or more in the presence of the Lord were absorbingly incredible! Even though it seemed I was at the altar for only a few minutes, *Time in His presence seemed to stand still!* What a miracle!

As hard as I have tried to describe what happened that New Year's Day, it was more spectacular and splendid than you can imagine!

DON'T LET THE VISION VANISH

On the way home in the car, I shared with my family some of the most impossible things that I had encountered in the vision. After we got home that New Year's morning, I decided to write down the things I remembered that happened in my vision. I realized I could not let this unique vision vanish as if it had not occurred. I had never experienced a vision before this event took place.

I knew I had to invest in writing it down while it was still fresh in my mind.

One of the greatest blessings I celebrated from my vision was what I call the "Divine Exchange." I had been rescued from *the ugly hands of destruction* that once held me captive…into *the Beautiful Loving Hands of the Lord,* which had set me free from bondage!

PROOF OF BEING IN LOVE WITH JESUS

After such a long and active night, I did not wake up until that afternoon on New Year's Day. Yet excited about my supernatural conversion, I started making calls to say Happy New Year's to others and to tell them about my new transformation.

The first person I decided to call was my best friend, Joyce. I also wanted to see if Jonathan was alright, especially after the bully had threatened us with a knife and a gang had been waiting to ambush us by standing at each end of the alley.

Well, I called Joyce with great anticipation of sharing my good news. However, there was no answer. But it was not unusual for Joyce's phone to ring multiple times. Sometimes, her father would not let them talk on the phone if their chores were not done. Although I called multiple times that day, I *never* got an answer. Eventually, my attempts to reach her turned into days, then weeks.

Unfortunately, I did not make contact with her until many years later. ***I did not know the last time we hugged at her house would be the last time I would see my best friend until well into our adulthood.*** (*Romans 8:28*) *And we know that all things work together for good to them that love God, to them who are the called according to His purpose.* I did not question God concerning the well-being of my friends. I had prayed for them, and I just believed that everything had turned out alright.

Nevertheless, I continued calling my extended family members, other friends, and old acquaintances to say, ***"Happy New Year and Happy New Me!"*** I was totally and completely excited about being made *brand new*, and this thing did not wear off; it wore in! I knew I was transformed because: I had a new positive mindset; my thinking had changed; my appetite for life had changed; I went from pitiful to joyful!

I was so excited! I could not wait to get back to school after the holiday break. I wanted everyone I knew to have the same opportunity to fall in love with Jesus! I felt like I had to tell my story. So, I hit the ground running, telling "The Greatest Story of My Life!" I was anxious and overjoyed to talk with everyone about my rescue and deliverance from sin through the love of Jesus Christ!

I began sharing my story everywhere I went, whether with the people at the grocery store, at school, on the bus, on the streets, or even at church. It became especially important for me to reach out to those who just seemed to be going to church as though it were just some kind of ritual. I remembered when I was in that broken state of mind while going to church every week. So it was important to me to reach out to as many young people in church as possible to tell them of the *Transforming Love of God!*

Instantly, I learned that true love for Jesus and for the people will make you bold, even if you are shy! I had no fear! This new boldness was the result of the complete transformation of the Holy Spirit in my life. *(Romans 1:16) For, we are not ashamed of the gospel of Christ, for it is the power of God unto salvation to everyone that believeth.*

Now, instead of looking for someone to **be my friend**, I decided **to be a friend** to nearly everyone I met. This approach to being a friend became **my outreach assignment.** Everybody needs a friend; I had experienced that firsthand. Now I was able to share with others about the friend I found in Jesus!

As I told my story, at the high school, people began to listen and started bringing others to me so I could tell them my story, too. **My story is the miracle of salvation,** and being born again is the miracle of His love for me!

Surprisingly, my popularity grew just because I loved Jesus and boldly proclaimed His name. I reached out to people in my conversations and with my caring manner.

I talked about how much God loved all of His children and that He wanted a special personal relationship with each of them. The young people heard me and started pulling up extra chairs to the table at lunchtime to hear me talk about the gospel of Jesus Christ! The space around the lunchroom table only seated 8 people, but on any given day, there would be 13–15 chairs surrounding my lunchroom table.

Amazingly, this was the same lunchroom table that I was sitting at when I was alone. Before my spiritual encounter with the Lord, I sat alone in the corner at this lunchroom table. I was shy, and I did not know anyone. Occasionally, I spoke to people who spoke to me.

But look how God turned everything around for His Glory! God had put so much love into me that I was just *OVERFLOWING!*

Now, how awesome is that?

The young people were getting saved, and they were requesting prayer and coming back with testimonies of victory and miracles! God showed himself strong because of our faith in Him.

This was the best fun I'd ever had in my 14 years of life! I was enjoying myself, talking about my love relationship with Jesus! I was absolutely bubbling over with the joy of the Lord! And guess what? I still enjoy talking about my love relationship with my Lord and Savior, Jesus Christ! And yes, I continue to bubble over with joy, even now!

What God started in me that New Year's Eve night

continues to grow within me for His Glory! The devil tried to destroy me that night at the party! ***But God had a plan for my life!*** *(Isa 29:11) For I know the plans I have for you, declares the Lord, "plans to prosper you and not to harm you, plans to give you hope and a future."*

The Lord knew it was time for me to make a decision for my future. I was picked out to be picked on so I could come to the brink of making a choice. ***There are always two choices: to follow the world or to follow Jesus Christ.*** I am so glad I decided to make Jesus my choice! I found out it was the best choice I could have ever made for my future.

T.A.G.

During those young years of being a bold witness for the Lord, he gave me a simple plan. The plan was to **TAG** everyone I came in contact with. The acronyms mean: **T**alk **A**bout **G**od... **T**hink **A**bout **God...** tell the **Truth About G**od… and to be... **T**hrilled **A**bout **G**od!

This plan was so simple. And I used every opportunity I got to **T**ell (my story) **A**bout **G**od! Through the years, many of the people who were touched by my story about the transforming Love of God now have wonderful stories of their own. They became witnesses for Christ, Soul-Winners, Ministers, and a few even became Pastors. *"To God Be The Glory!"*

The results were amazing. Many souls were added to the kingdom of God because of the boldness of one little 14-year-old girl! Yes! That little girl, at one time, was looking to find love in the wrong people. I was so shattered and broken from the devastation of molestation. But in the midst of the search for love, healing, and acceptance, *I found true love* and genuine acceptance through Salvation, and a life-changing relationship through Jesus Christ.

I am thankful to the Lord that "*He Brought Me: From Shattered Glass, To A Fashioned Diamond!* This one line is my ultimate defining story!

*(Malachi 3:16-17) Then those who feared the Lord **talked often one to another,** and the Lord listened and heard it, and a book of remembrance was written before Him of those who reverenced and worshipfully feared the Lord and that thought on His name. 17) "And they shall be mine, says the Lord of hosts, in that day when I publicly recognize and openly declare them to be **My Jewels (my special possession, a peculiar treasure).***

Praise the Lord! I humbly acknowledge that I am

one of the **Precious Jewels,** today. After much thought, *I chose to identify my process with that of the diamond.*

DIAMONDS ARE FOREVER

When I think of the vision, I remember so many unpleasant things that the Lord delivered me from, as well as the many pleasant and awesome things he transformed me into. I declared that as God was putting something beautiful inside of me, He was also taking something ugly out of me!

I vividly remembered that I went through a variety of events and stages that progressively cleansed and purified me in the vision. Through the process, God made sure I was aware of the series and the changes that I went through because each level progressively intensified.

Now, when I look back, I feel that He put me through the same kind of changes you would in order to make a diamond! First, He pulled me out of the obscure place of dirt and mud to a place of cleansing because He loved me. I was put under God's magnifying, illuminating light of healing and forgiveness as I was being transformed.

That powerful, supernatural x-ray beam of light not only exposed the impurities that were in my life, but at the same time it was pressing out all the ugly mess. While God was making and sculpting me into His very best! With the purifying light of His love, He showed me extreme, brilliant lights, intense heat, and multiple jolts of heavy fire penetrating through my body as He purged me! Finally, I was ready to go up the Fiery Ladder, (which to me represents the Holy Spirit) to be touched by the awesome Hands of Jesus!

There is a saying that **"Diamonds Are Forever."** Why? Because of the high degree of fire, the intense pressure, and the multiple stages of processing that the diamond goes through before it becomes an invincible, rare, and priceless stone.

The diamond is known for its endurance even before it can be called a pure diamond. Yet, it goes through more intense fire to burn out any impurities that may be hidden. Only then is the diamond ready to be cut and perfected in the master's skillful hands. It is the master's craftsmanship that brings out the extraordinary, rare beauty and quality that exist in the deep crevices of this phenomenal treasure. *The deeper the cut, the more brilliantly it sparkles!*

Praise the Lord! A true diamond was made, fashioned, and transformed in God's presence. It was as if, step by step, stage by stage, I was progressively being formed and made brand new by the power of the Holy Spirit! That's when I knew I had been reborn, changed, converted, and made into something more wonderful and valuable than I could have ever imagined.

Now, as I look back, I can see that each of the lessons learned in the supernatural vision had already taken root on the inside of me. My life was changed before I got up off the floor in the little Pentecostal church.

These are precious memories that I continuously hold near and dear to my heart.

Even though many years have passed since my ultimate, life-changing spiritual encounter with my Lord and Savior, Jesus Christ, the impact has not worn off! Hallelujah! I was forever changed!

I am so grateful to God that I repented. The Lord loved me enough to forgive me. Then He fashioned and created me into something new and precious for His Glory! *(2 Corinthians 5:17) Therefore, if anyone is in Christ, he is a new creation; old things have passed away; behold, all things have become new.*

It was through the process that I became new, and I learned to say, **"Yes, *Lord! I* continue to say, *Yes, Lord! And It Is Forever: Yes, Lord, in My Heart!"***

"Diamonds May Be Forever! But God's Fashioned Diamonds Are Forever, Saying... Yes, Lord!!!

God's Overflowing Love is yet causing people's lives to be fashioned, converted, and changed into glorious lights that do sparkle and shine: "These are God's Precious Diamonds, Gems, and Jewels Shining for His Glory!"

(Matt 5:16) Let your light so shine before men, that they may see your good works and glorify your Father, which is in heaven.

PERSONAL REFLECTIONS CONCERNING
CHAPTER 5

Chapter Five gives an account of what happened in Chapter Four. No doubt, change has actually taken place, and there are witnesses, signs, and evidence.

1. When you experience something special in your life, it is always good to have a witness. An eyewitness account comes from a different point of view.

2. Have you ever been somewhere and lost track of the time and you were bewildered as to what happened?

3. Sometimes, in the presence of the Lord, time seems to stand still. Have you ever had the feeling that God had you in a holding place so He could get your attention?

4. Have you ever been in a powerful anointed service, where it seemed like everyone was getting blessed? If so, please take time to reflect.

5. I've heard it said, "Love is in the details." Can you remember the details of your testimony and your transformation? If so, take time to recall those precious moments

or to write them down. It will bless you.

6. Do you have a strong desire to *talk about God* with others? Are you afraid to talk about God with others? Do you TAG with other Christians?

7. It's time to let your light **SHINE!** Because God's precious jewels do let their light shine. They carry the glorious light of the Gospel within them everywhere they go. *Don't be afraid to let your light shine!*

All scripture is taken from King James Version
Bible, unless otherwise noted.

Psalm 16:11
Thou wilt shew me the path of life: in thy presence
is fullness of joy; at thy right hand there are
pleasures forevermore.

Romans 8:28
And we know that all things work together for good
to them that love God, to them who are the called
according to his purpose.

Romans 1:16
For I am not ashamed of the gospel of Christ: for it
is the power of God unto salvation to everyone that
believeth…

Malachi 3:16-17
And they shall be Mine, says the Lord of hosts, in
that day when I publicly recognize and openly
declare them to be My Jewels (My peculiar
treasure). And I will spare them, as a man spares
his own son who serves him. AMPC

2 Corinthians 5:17
Therefore, if anyone is in Christ, he is a new
creation; old things have passed away; behold, all
things have become new. NKJV

Matthew 5:16

Let your light so shine before men, that they may see your good works, and glorify your Father which is in heaven.

CHAPTER SIX

FROM SHATTERED
TO HEALED

BEWARE: DON'T GET CAUGHT IN-BETWEEN

There are many people who are like my family, as I
mentioned in Chapter 1. We served the church well,
but we were not serving God well. We were faithful
to the church, but we were not faithful to God. We
were dedicated to what we were doing, but we were
not as dedicated to the Word of God. We were good
church-going people who said we were Christians.
As I stated before, "Going into a church does not
make you a Christian any more than going into a
garage makes you a car." *But because of our half-
heartedness, we were unknowingly unprepared for
heaven. We were followers of good, but we were
not true followers of Jesus Christ. Could you
possibly be making the same mistake?*

Serving God is not about the bricks and mortar of

the building that you attend for service. ***But serving God is about the sincerity and true commitment of your heart to Him.***

As a teenager, I was involved with the church weekly, but I was also involved with my worldly friends daily. I lacked a true commitment to God. I did not understand that salvation was about making a choice. I was fired up about singing in the choir, but not as fired up about proclaiming Jesus as my Savior. God cannot tolerate phonies, hypocrites, or Mr. or Ms. In-Betweens. I was not all-in with God, nor was I all-in with the world. I was somewhere in between.

One of the most crucial scriptures in the Bible that many people overlook as if it does not exist is *(Revelation 3:15–16). Jesus said, "I know all the things you do, that you are neither hot nor cold. I wish you were one or the other! 16) But since you are like lukewarm water, I will spit (vomit) you out of my mouth!"*

I still get chills whenever I read this scripture because many people are going through the motions of being Christians. Many are committed to the church but not to the Christ of the church. Beware of being caught in between!

God does not stop loving you because you are cold

or lukewarm toward Him. But you deny yourself and him the opportunity for a true, godly relationship. God is looking for a pure heart. He cannot endure the one who is lukewarm or just in-between. It makes him sick.

But if you desire a powerful (true-hot) spiritually strong relationship with the Lord, here's what to do: (James 1:21-22) Get rid of all the filth and the evil in your lives, repent, and humbly accept the word God has planted in your hearts, for it has the power to save your souls. 22) But don't just listen to God's word. You must do what it says. Otherwise, you are only fooling yourselves.

JESUS IS GOD'S EXCLAMATION MARK OF HIS DIVINE LOVE!

Mankind had sinned continuously in the face of a loving God. Death was the penalty that mankind deserved. *But "God's Love" intentionally got in the way! (John 3:16-17) For God so greatly loved and dearly prized the world that He [even] gave His [one and only] begotten Son, so that whoever believes and trusts in Him [as Savior] shall not perish but have eternal life. 17) For God did not send His Son into the world to judge and condemn it, but that the world might be saved through Him.*

God sent help to us because He loved us so much that He sacrificed His one and Only Son! He did this so sinners could be saved, so shattered people could be healed, and so that broken people could be put back together again. And people who thought life had nothing to offer could feel valued! The love of God transcends every barrier of the enemy when we call on Him out of a sincere heart! (*Romans 10:10*) *For it is by believing in your heart that you are made right with God, and it is by openly declaring your faith that you are saved.*

"Repentance is not about the severity of your sin, but the sincerity of your heart!"

Your life is too wonderful for you to throw it away! The hand of the Lord is already on your life if you are reading this awesome *journey of healing.* The battle has started within you to continue the way you were before you picked up this book. But you know the Lord is calling you, as He did me in the vision. He was calling me to come to Him.

THIS IS YOUR TIME!

God is calling you to come to Him and to turn your life around for the better. All you have to do is humbly open your heart, ask Him for forgiveness of your past sins, and simply say, "Yes, Lord, I want a true relationship with you now. I have put you off long enough; I realize I need you in my life!"

GOD HAS A VERY SPECIAL PLAN FOR YOUR LIFE!

The bottom line is that the devil wants you dead; he wants you unhappy, broken, or shattered to pieces. This enemy and thief does not care how young or old you are; his plan of action is to destroy you. (John 10:9-10) Jesus said, "I am the way. Those who come in through me will be saved. 10) The thief's purpose is to steal, kill, and destroy. My purpose is to give them a rich and satisfying life."

There was a time in my life when I needed a Savior, but I was seeking a friend instead. So the enemy tried to destroy me through broken relationships and phony friends.

It was at the most vulnerable point in my life that I was feeling rejected, worthless, and unaccepted. I was then attacked and assaulted by a molester being used by the devil. The plan of the enemy was to ultimately destroy my life and my future.

But God, in His grace, mercy, and love, touched me and gave me a heart of repentance. Instead of being bitter, angry, and revengeful, I chose to come to God with all my troubles and repent of my sins. I asked God to help me overcome the spirit of oppression, fear, and torment! The Lord forgave me, delivered me, and healed me!

Yes, God did it! It was the true love of God that turned things around in the midst of my crisis! At that time, I was running away from God when suddenly I realized just how much I needed Him. *"Help, Lord!" was my heart's cry when He heard me and forgave me.* *(Romans 10:13)* *Everyone who calls on the name of the Lord will be saved.* (Please revisit chapters 2–3 of this book for more details.)

My precious ones: *Don't let this moment pass you by!* I thought I would always be a victim because of what happened to me. But the love of God, through His tender mercies, made me victorious instead!

THIS IS YOUR TIME TO BE HEALED, MY SISTER OR BROTHER, NOW!

This is your time to let go of the hurt, the shame, and the ugly stuff that you regret happening to you or someone close to you! You cannot undo what has shattered you. But you can stop the madness of the torment that is trying to keep you in bondage and shackled to your past. *(Matt 11:28-29) Then Jesus said, "Come to me, all of you who are weary*

*and carry heavy burdens, and I will give you rest.
29) Take my yoke upon you. Let me teach you,
because I am humble and gentle, and you will find
rest for your souls.*

I know it is because of God's grace and mercy that I
am saved today. You see, I came to the Lord out of
fear, but I stayed with the Lord out of love! I fell in
love with God, and I fell in love with His Word.
God is love, and Jesus is the Word. *(John 1:14) So
the Word (Jesus) became human and made his
home among us. He was full of unfailing love and
faithfulness.*

**I FOUND OUT THAT THE ONLY WAY TO TRULY
SERVE GOD IS TO TRULY LOVE HIM!**

*(1 John 4:8–9) But anyone who does not love does
not know God, for God is love. 9 God showed how
much he loved us by sending his only Son (Jesus)
into the world so that we might have eternal life
through him.*

To experience and know the love of God is such a
miraculous, extraordinary happening that cannot be
denied! The awesome power of God's love
transcends to the very core of your inner man at the
exact moment you truly surrender your heart to
Him. *(1 John 1:9) If we confess our sins, he is
faithful and just and will forgive us our sins and*

purify us from all unrighteousness.

With all that has been said or written, ***the time has come for you to make a choice!*** Will you accept God's remedy for your hurt and pain? I spoke to you from the chambers of my heart about my pain. And I have shared with you the ultimate victory and transformation that took place after I came to Jesus with all my brokenness and all my baggage. "I am so glad the Lord loved me enough to rescue me!"

BUT NOW, THE LORD IS WAITING ON YOU TO ACCEPT HIS HEALING FOR YOUR SOUL!

Take a moment to think about your personal and spiritual needs as you reverently approach a "Holy God" who already loves you. ***Yes, God already loves you! But God does not tolerate sin, now or ever!*** This is why we must repent of our sins, turn away from them, and sincerely give our hearts to love and serve the Lord Jesus!

THE PRAYER OF REPENTANCE

Have mercy on me, O God, because of your unfailing love. Because of your great compassion, blot out the stain of my sins. Wash me clean from my guilt. Purify me from my sins, and I will be clean; wash me, and I will be whiter than snow. (Psalm 51:1-2).

Lord, I acknowledge that I need you in my life to make a brand new start. Now, Lord Jesus, heal me from my past and present wounds. I invite you to come into my heart, live in me, and make something beautiful of my life for your glory! Amen! Amen!! Amen!!!

In the words of Jesus to one who was forgiven, *"Go, and sin no more!"* (*John 8:11) And Jesus said, "Neither do I condemn thee; go, and sin no more."*

Believe that God has heard your prayer and that you have been set free! Praise the Lord! (PTL)

By faith, receive forgiveness; walk in the fact that God has healed you from the sin, hurt, pain, and shame. Praise the Lord often by telling Him, "*Thank you for setting me free!"*

Now, develop a *daily lifestyle of prayer* by talking to the Lord. Take a pen and paper with you when you pray. Stay in the Lord's presence long enough for the Holy Spirit to speak to your heart. It may be a scripture, or the love of God may reveal something to you to share with others. *Write it down*! This is very important because the devil will try to make you forget what God put on your heart.

Next: Start *reading your Bible for survival.* If you

don't know where to start reading, go back through the pages of this book and read the scripture reference pages at the end of each chapter. The Word of God will teach you how to put the Lord first in your life!

VICTORIOUS PRINCIPLES TO LIVE BY

I learned some valuable principles to live by from my vision, which helped me stay on track:

1. Faith in God will simply help you through whatever you may face. Just trust him.

2. Love the Lord with all your heart, and choose to serve Him as you receive His love daily. (It's all or nothing; no Mr. or Ms. In-Between.)

3. Obey His Word and follow His instructions as you are being transformed.

4. Rest in His arms, and don't doubt. He will not leave you or forsake you.

5. Arise to a "Brand New Life," to a new you, and to a new relationship with Jesus Christ!

Walk confidently in your newfound faith. Enjoy your time in God's presence as you go through these "Victorious Principles to Live By."

WELCOME TO A "BRAND NEW LIFE" IN JESUS CHRIST!

TODAY: YOU ARE NEITHER SHATTERED NOR BROKEN...

TODAY... YOU ARE HEALED!!!

Continue rejoicing for the victory you have received in your life! Now you can tell your story of victory to others, so someone else can be healed and blessed!

Why did God allow all of this to happen to me? My response is, *"So I could tell my story to those who need to hear, how I came from being shattered to being healed!* Also, how I came from being unaccepted to being a mouthpiece for those who needed a friend and a Savior. *(2 Corinthians 1:4) God comforts us in all our troubles so that we can comfort others.*

I tell people I came to Jesus out of fear, but I stayed with Him out of love. Today, His love still fines me, refines me, designs me, and assigns me to tell others about His Life-Changing Love!

Since then, many more visions and outreach programs have been implemented to rescue souls for the glory of God through the ministry. But the greatest assignment that He gave me that we can all do is the outreach ministry of love by simply sharing "*Our Story!*"

The world is waiting to hear your awesome story of the magnificent love of Jesus Christ, and how He healed and rescued you!

TAG! Tell About God!

"NOW, GO TELL YOUR STORY FOR GOD'S GLORY!"

GOD IS TRULY AMAZING!!!

A SPECIAL NOTE: As I shared the five victorious principles from my vision that got me through victoriously, I did not see that the order of the acronyms literally spelled out my name. I was surprised when God revealed it to me while I was typing. I went back and underlined so you could see too. *How awesome is that! It's just a little bonus to let me know, He's Still Truly Amazing!!!*

All scripture is taken from the King James Version Bible unless otherwise noted.

Rev 3:15-16
Jesus said, "I know all the things you do, that you are neither hot nor cold. I wish you were one or the other! 16) But since you are like lukewarm water, I will spit (vomit) you out of my mouth! NLT

James 1:21-22
So, get rid of all the filth and the evil in your lives, (repent), and humbly accept the word God has planted in your hearts, for it has the power to save your souls. 22) But don't just listen to God's word. You must do what it says. Otherwise, you are only fooling yourselves. NLT

John 3:16-17
For God so greatly loved and dearly prized the world that He [even] gave His [One and] only begotten Son, so that whoever believes and trusts in Him, [as Savior] shall not perish, but have eternal life. 17) For God did not send the (His) Son into the world to judge and condemn the world… but that the world might be saved through Him. AMP

Romans 10:10
For it is by believing in your heart that you are

made right with God, and it is by openly declaring your faith that you are saved. NLT

John 10:9-10
Jesus said: Yes, I am the (way) gate. Those who come in through me will be saved… 10) The thief's purpose is to steal and kill and destroy. My purpose is to give them (you) a rich and satisfying life. NLT

Romans 10:13
"Everyone who calls on the name of the Lord will be saved." NLT

2 Corinthians 1:4
(God) He comforts us in all our troubles so that we can comfort others… NLT

Matt 11:28-29
Jesus said, "Come to me, all of you who are weary and carry heavy burdens, and I will give you rest. 29) Take my yoke upon you. Let me teach you, because I am humble and gentle, and you will find rest for your souls. NLT

1 John 4:8-9
But anyone who does not love does not know God — for God is Love. 9) God showed how much he loved us by sending his only Son into the world so that we might have eternal life through Him. NLT

John 1:14

So the Word became human and made His home among us. He was full of unfailing love and faithfulness. And we have seen his glory, the glory of the Father's one and only Son. NLT

1 John 1:9

If we confess our sins, he is faithful and just and will forgive us our sins and purify us from all unrighteousness. NIV

Ps 51:1-2, 7

Have mercy on me, O God, because of your unfailing love. Because of your great compassion, blot out the stain of my sins. 2) Wash me clean from my guilt. Purify me from my sins, 7) and I will be clean; wash me, and I will be whiter than snow. NLT

John 8:11

…And Jesus said to her, "Neither do I condemn you; go and sin no more." NKJV

My Favorite Scripture: (Galatians 2:20) I am crucified with Christ nevertheless I live; yet not I but Christ liveth within me. And the life which I now live in the flesh I live by the faith of the Son of God, who loved me and gave himself for me.

WORDS OF ENDORSEMENT & ENCOURAGEMENT

COMMENTS-WORDS OF ENCOURAGEMENT:

Flora is not only an awesome woman of God, but she is also my mother. Many people affectionately call her Prophetess, Mama J, Mama Flo, and other names of endearment. However, I have the privilege of calling her Momma!

A mother of two beautiful daughters, my mom raised us by her example. She was saved everywhere she went, and she was saved at home! I remember some nights waking up to her voice. I'd look at the foot of my bed, and there she was, praying and warring for me in prayer...covering me with the blood of Jesus and destroying any assignments of the devil.

Momma has mentored many people because of her close walk with God, her Christian guidance, and her example. She is the reason I, my children, and many of my friends are saved today! *I truly thank God that He gave me you as a mother...I love you Momma and I am so proud of you!*

-Pastor Shawn A. Jackson/Clark,
(Your baby girl) Joliet, IL

Flora Jackson is called many things; Mother, Daughter, Sister, Grammy, Friend, Prophetess and Evangelist. For me, as I am sure I can speak for so many of her other spiritual daughters and sons, I lovingly call her **Mama J.** She has been my spiritual mentor who cheered me when I got "it" right and corrected me when I didn't. She walked beside me during the good and the challenging times, always providing nuggets of wisdom from the Word and a ready prayer that reached the throne room of God. When I look at this woman of God, I see the love of God exuding from her. She is indeed love in action. Flora Jackson is a: Lover of God, Handmaiden of God, and Extraordinary Teacher of the Word, Intercessor, Mentor, Counselor, Encourager and an Influencer.

She is a PRECIOUS GIFT from God to this world.

-Elder Anita F. Muse,
(aka: Her Velcro Daughter)- Meridianville, Alabama

How often do you meet a person through someone else, and they become your friend for life? Flo and I met when in our 20's, and that was many years ago. Many people thought we were biological sisters, because we looked alike and had so much in common. Although living in different states, we loved, shared and supported each other through the good times as well as the times that were not so good! I've always admired her love for and commitment to God! Under her leadership, I have

147

attended and participated in meetings and special events for the "**United Christian Women of America**." For the last fourteen plus years, I've continued to be blessed each month by her leadership with "**Love Overflowing Ministries.**"

-Missionary/Evangelist Beverly Johnson,
Milwaukee, Wisconsin-

Ms. Flora, you are an awesome woman of God. I admire your faith, your strength, and your love for others. You have truly been a blessing in my life!

Love, Blessings & God's Grace,
-Gwen Sims,
Chicago, IL (Workplace Friend)

I met Flora as a teenager (many years) ago. She was the co-lead youth leader or pastor for our youth group, she was about 16 years old. At that time, she mentored me from a distance. Her depth and transparent walk with the Lord inspired me to want a more personal relationship with Him. Years passed, and a one-on-one relationship emerged after graduating from college, marrying, and having my first child as a young mom. *Sometimes, a moment will connect hearts, and divine relationships are* *founded.* I was privileged to have Pastor Flora Jackson as my mentor, and *our journey together forever changed my life.*

Flora began a ministry called **"UNITED CHRISTIAN WOMEN of AMERICA."** We would meet at her home. There would be such a mighty move of God. We began to refer to these times as "A One Night Revival." These one-night revivals were a clarion call to women from various walks of life. Some were brand new to the faith, with habits and hang-ups that needed to be broken, and some women had known and walked with the Lord for years. **God did miracles** in that very intimate space and meshed our lives together. Women were delivered from drugs and destructive lifestyles and released from toxic relationships. Women were endowed with the power of the Holy Spirit to live free from the bondages that had imprisoned them for years. The lives of many were changed because of the ministry of, "The United Christian Women of America!"

Love you!
-Linda Gordon-

(Positive Behavior Intervention & Support Coach for Alternative High Schools) **Mather, California**

My godmother, Flora Jackson, aka "Mama J," aka "Mama Prophetess," has been a constant in my life for many years. Our relationship began when she invited me to stay overnight at her home – a night that changed me forever. I was in a broken place, convinced that I had failed God and doubtful that my life could ever be anything of value to Him. Elder Jackson, as she was called then, didn't lecture me or ask me any questions. Instead, *she shared her story with me*. She shared her testimony of how the Lord saved her as a young girl, the difference He made in her life, and the love relationship she had cultivated with Jesus, the Lover of her soul! She talked about her passion for prayer, the simplicity of talking to God and letting Him talk back. She spoke about the power of God's Word! I was changing with every hour that passed. *That night, God set me free! Both Mama J and I knew that I was different.* She said I went through a complete metamorphosis that night; and she started calling me *Butterfly*. I had found my voice and my identity in Jesus, and my life would never be the same.

Since that time, I've had the honor of watching this powerful woman's walk with God. I've heard her preach the house down. I've seen God work miracles of healing and deliverance through her.

I am forever grateful for the story she shared with me years ago, the story she is now choosing to share with the world. Now more than ever, the world needs to hear about the simplicity of falling in love with Jesus and the power and victory that comes with allowing Him to simply live through us. **Your life will truly be blessed as you journey through the pages of this book!**

– Prophetess Toni R. Harris, (aka Prophetess Jr.)
Aurora, IL

A SPECIAL THANK YOU:

To my wonderful family and friends who have supported me on this new journey of faith into a new assignment.

Your beautiful words have lifted me higher, and I trust those who read your wonderful comments, will be uplifted, too.

My heart is overflowing with much love and gratitude.

I appreciate the many responses. However, I am only able to include a few. I love you, honor you, and respect you. Each word you have written is precious, and priceless to me! Thank you so much for your well-wishes and prayers!

Flora,

Thank you Lord, for All You Have Done, God, I Give You the Glory!

www.ingramcontent.com/pod-product-compliance
Lightning Source LLC
Chambersburg PA
CBHW071942100426
42737CB00046BA/1816